# Once Upon a Rhyme

## Norfolk & Suffolk
### Edited by Debbie Killingworth

First published in Great Britain in 2011 by:

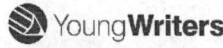

Young Writers
Remus House
Coltsfoot Drive
Peterborough
PE2 9BF
Telephone: 01733 890066
Website: www.youngwriters.co.uk

All Rights Reserved
Book Design by Tim Christian
© Copyright Contributors 2011
SB ISBN 978-0-85739-483-5

THIS BOOK BELONGS TO

..............................................

# Foreword

Here at Young Writers our objective is to help children discover the joys of poetry and creative writing. Few things are more encouraging for the aspiring writer than seeing their own work in print. We are proud that our anthologies are able to give young authors this unique sense of confidence and pride in their abilities.

Once Upon A Rhyme is our latest fantastic competition, specifically designed to encourage the writing skills of primary school children through the medium of poetry. From the high quality of entries received, it is clear that Once Upon A Rhyme really captured the imagination of all involved.

The resulting collection is an excellent showcase for the poetic talents of the younger generation and we are sure you will be charmed and inspired by it, both now and in the future.

# Contents

*Maddie Stewart is our featured poet this year. She has written a nonsense workshop for you and included some of her great poems. You can find these at the end of your book.*

### Bramfield House School, Bramfield
Joshua Wilkins (10) ..................... 1
Ethan Baker (11) ......................... 1

### Foulsham Primary School, Foulsham
Harry Wright (9) .......................... 1
Saffron Hedges (10) .................... 2
Millie Notley (10) ......................... 3
Abigail Cater (10) ....................... 4
Mae Betts (10) ............................ 5
Callum Pell (11) .......................... 6
Hollie Godfrey (11) ..................... 7
Danielle Nabarro (9) ................... 8
Abbie Watts (9) .......................... 9
Sam Bush (10) .......................... 10
Max Wright (11) ........................ 10
Jordan Day (10) ........................ 11
Bethan Levesley (9) .................. 11
Anna Sinclair (10) ..................... 12
Abigail Burnham (11) ................ 13
Abbie Claxton (11) .................... 14
Callum Bowen-Jones (10) ........ 15
Lexie Cox (11) .......................... 16
Finlay Bond (11) ....................... 16
Reece Nabarro (11) .................. 17
Finley Castell (10) .................... 17
Dylan Hann (10) ....................... 18
Megan Hales (10) ..................... 18
Austin Searjeant (9) .................. 19
Abbie Colman (10) ................... 19

### Great Massingham CE Primary School, Great Massingham
Courtney Burton (8) .................. 20
Troy Bolt (10) ............................ 21
Charlie Reeve (9) ..................... 22
Nicholas Stanley (10) ............... 22
Adam Clarke (11) ..................... 23
Lucy Barlow (9) ........................ 23
Conner Curson (8) ................... 24
Tigga Aldiss (8) ........................ 24
Bethany Gibson-Hill (11) .......... 25
Kimberley Cooper (10) ............. 25
Ellie Overson (7) ...................... 26
Louise Clarke (7) ...................... 26
Luke Fryett (10) ........................ 26
Chloe Harper (9) ...................... 27

### Hainford Primary Partnership School, Hainford
Maisie Bale (8) ......................... 27
Olivia Hill (9) ............................. 27
Bradley Constable (8) .............. 28
Adam Sarsby (9) ...................... 28
Joseph Veriod (9) ..................... 28
Matthew Germany (10) ............. 29
Chloe McMullon (8) .................. 29
Leestefan Drake (10) ............... 29
Lily Bates (8) ............................ 30
Helena Mellows (9) .................. 30
Scott Harwood (8) .................... 30
Ryan Watker (9) ....................... 31

Andrew Howes (9) .......................................... 31
Francesca Le Mesurier (10) ...................... 31
Georgia Stannett (9) .................................... 32
Cole Snowling-Dunford (8) ......................... 32
Ellen Baker-Breame (9) ............................... 32
James Lord (9) ............................................. 32

## Hardwick Primary School, Bury St Edmunds
Chloe Sparks (8) .......................................... 33
Ellie Parker (8) .............................................. 33
Benjamin Foreman (9) ................................. 33

## Hevingham Primary School, Hevingham
Maisie Robinson (8) .................................... 34
Libby Field (9) ............................................... 34
Olivia Bullen (8) ............................................ 35
Cameron Earnshaw (9) ............................... 35
Ethan Glynn (8) ............................................ 35
Marcie Mitchell (8) ....................................... 36
Conor Glynn (8) ............................................ 36
Jack Ferizi (9) ............................................... 36
Evie Cowling (7) ........................................... 37
Thomas Lake (7) .......................................... 37

## Horning Community Primary School, Horning
Zack Frosdick (10) ....................................... 37
Lily Brittle (10) ............................................... 38
Jordan Evans (10) ........................................ 38
Amy Crockford (11) ...................................... 39
James Willoughby (8) .................................. 39
George Frosdick (8) .................................... 40
George Echlin-Riches (9) ........................... 40
Jordan Hayton (10) ...................................... 41
Auguste Jones (9) ........................................ 41
India Everett (8) ............................................ 41

## Kelsale CE (VC) Primary School, Kelsale
Evie Salter (8) ............................................... 42
Maxwell Moore (8) ....................................... 42
Madeline Salter (8) ...................................... 43
Jenny Roberts (7) ........................................ 43
Jamie Roberts (9) ........................................ 44
Grace Pelekanou (8) ................................... 44
Bradley Eagle (8) ......................................... 44

Grace Watts (8) ............................................ 45
Megan Enticknap ......................................... 45
Poppy Stone (9) ........................................... 45
Myah Ridgeon (8) ........................................ 46
Sophie Ross (8) ........................................... 46
Fynley Hoyland (8) ....................................... 46
Grace Tanton Brown (7) .............................. 47
Cameron Ling (7) ......................................... 47
Aaron Nelhams (8) ...................................... 47
Andy Ball (9) ................................................. 47
Bethany Hall (8) ........................................... 48
Bethany Warren (8) ..................................... 48
Amy Rowe (7) ............................................... 48
Scott Brown (7) ............................................ 48
Cameron Buckle (8) .................................... 49

## Middleton VC Primary School, Middleton
Kloii Hood (10) .............................................. 49
Shannon Tinkler (9) ..................................... 49
Lauryn Bland (11) ........................................ 50
Scarlet-Lilli Cooke (10) ............................... 51
Saffron Kirkpatrick (10) ............................... 51
Benjamin Brandes (9) ................................. 52
Emma Brandes (10) .................................... 52
Emily Holland (11) ....................................... 53
Aaron Williamson (10) ................................. 53
Matthew Daw (10) ........................................ 53
Alex Florance (10) ....................................... 54
Jack George (10) ......................................... 54
Lucy-May Whitear (9) .................................. 54
Harvey Rae (10) ........................................... 55
Harry Daw (10) ............................................. 55
Bronte Rose (10) ......................................... 55
Chloe Marks (10) ......................................... 56
James Taylor (10) ........................................ 56
Billie Rust (11) .............................................. 56
Lynsey Marks (9) ......................................... 57
Hannah Evans (9) ........................................ 57
Tommy Wilson (11) ...................................... 57
Sophie Bland (10) ........................................ 58
Nick Peters (11) ........................................... 58

## Oulton Broad Primary School, Oulton Broad
Belinda Leech (10) ...................................... 58

Beth Scarlett (10) ........ 59
Hope Reynolds (7) ........ 59
Taylor Dyer-Jackman (10) ........ 60
Rebecca Mawer (9) ........ 61
Hannah Rogers (10) ........ 62
Harvey Farrow (8) ........ 62
Jack Townley (9) ........ 63
Rio Howard (7) ........ 63
Ella Cunningham (9) ........ 64
Aidan Curtis (8) ........ 64
Hannah Reid (9) ........ 65
Ethan Nicolle (8) ........ 65
Cameron Harbord (9) ........ 66
Adam Seager (7) ........ 66
Nathan Turrell (9) ........ 67
Sonny Anderson (8) ........ 67
Scarlet Banner (9) ........ 68
John McNamara (7) ........ 68
Kian Harvey (9) ........ 69
Jack Kirk (8) ........ 69
Amy Hoffman (9) ........ 70
Rebecca Braid (7) ........ 70
Deren Karausta (10) ........ 71
Thomas Riley (8) ........ 71
Harry Halstein (10) ........ 72
Erin Cook (7) ........ 72
Tia Smith (10) ........ 73
Robert Flower (10) ........ 73
Freya Easey (10) ........ 74
Caitlin Farr (10) ........ 74
Sophie Cooper (10) ........ 75
Emily Hall (9) ........ 75
Travis Jacobs (9) ........ 76
Josh Dixon (9) ........ 76
James Lawler (10) ........ 77
Philippa Parr (9) ........ 77
Tegan-Elise Warren-Patterson (7) ........ 78
Thomas Betts (8) ........ 78
Daniel Bowen (7) ........ 78
Ethan Schroder (7) ........ 79

### Redcastle Furze Primary School, Thetford
Jacob Cameron (11) ........ 79
Blossom May (8) ........ 80
Angel Lott (8) ........ 80

### St Felix School, Southwold
Sarah Watts (11) ........ 80
Imogen Templer (10) ........ 81
Sam Ellis (11) ........ 82
Ellie Heil (11) ........ 82
Grace Collen (10) ........ 83
May Bandy (11) ........ 83
Olivia Ellis (10) ........ 84
Natasha Harlock (9) ........ 84
James Harris (10) ........ 85
Ross Tolliday (10) ........ 85
Edward Paulley (10) ........ 86
Ava Jackson (9) ........ 86
Lucy Clarke (9) ........ 87
Edith McKenna (10) ........ 87
Joseph Drake (10) ........ 88
Harry Collins (10) ........ 88
Thomas Hood (10) ........ 89
Joseph Powell (9) ........ 89
Emily Summers (10) ........ 90
Archie Laughland (11) ........ 90
Madeleine Chambers (10) ........ 90
Sophie Keal (11) ........ 91
Thea Hall (10) ........ 91
Thomas Hill (10) ........ 91
Archie Wallis (11) ........ 92
Oliver Annis (9) ........ 92

### Seething & Mundham Primary School, Seething
Evelyn Howat (10) ........ 92
Amelia McIntyre (7) ........ 93
Emily Storey (7) ........ 93
Ryan Crowder-Barr (9) ........ 94
Eleanor Storey (9) ........ 94
Louis Price (9) ........ 94
Fenella Jenkins (10) ........ 94
Joshua Davies (10) ........ 95
Annabel Wykes (10) ........ 95
Lucy Mann (10) ........ 95
Siouxsie Littlewood (11) ........ 95
Esme Walton (8) ........ 96
Sam Warren (9) ........ 96
Arwen Proctor (7) ........ 96
Rory Jackson (8) ........ 96

## Weeting Primary School, Weeting
Julia Vickova (8) .......................... 97
Charlie Long (7) ........................... 97
Cara Solomon (11) ....................... 98
Ellie-May McCreedy (7) ............... 98
Gaby Holder (10) .......................... 99
Samantha Smith (10) ................... 99
Jordan Rhodes (9) ...................... 100
Chris Pope (11) ........................... 100
Emily Moore (11) ......................... 101
Danny Juniper (11) ...................... 101
Jessica Baker (10) ...................... 101
Alicia Drewry (10) ....................... 102
Max McCreedy (11) .................... 102
Destiny Back (10) ....................... 102
Libby Brockett (10) ..................... 103
Joseph Dilley (10) ....................... 103
Ryan Aves (10) ........................... 103
Lewis Wells (9) ........................... 104
Alicia Frost (11) .......................... 104
Naomi Hadnum (11) ................... 104
Charlie Stone (11) ...................... 105
Daniel Buonocore (11) ............... 105
Charles Smith (11) ..................... 105
Catalina Lis (10) ......................... 106
Eleanor Vaughan (7) .................. 106

## West Earlham Junior School, Norwich
Jordan Reader (10) .................... 106
James Goldie (10) ...................... 107
Rafa Nazim (7) ............................ 107
Rwanda Wilkerson (10) .............. 108
Whitney Dunthorne (10) ............. 109
Luke Chamberlain (11) ............... 110
Charmaine Storey (11) ............... 110
Joseph Kuta (10) ........................ 111
Wisdom Danns (10) .................... 111
Sinead Hoban (11) ..................... 112
Jessica Day (8) ........................... 112
Sarah Muhammad (7) ................ 113

## West Row Community Primary School, West Row
Ryan Surridge (8) ....................... 113
Aimee Flack (8) .......................... 114

Jack Merrill (8) ............................ 115
Brendan Price (7) ....................... 115
Lyndon Dozier (7) ....................... 116

## West Winch Primary School, King's Lynn
Laila Chaudhry (9) ...................... 116
Lily Davidson (8) ......................... 117
Dayna Edwards (8) ..................... 118
Millie Rattenbury (8) ................... 119
Joe Pearce (8) ............................ 120
Eknath Manoj (9) ........................ 120
Susannah Murray (8) .................. 121
Natasha Denney (9) ................... 121
Jasmine Reeve (8) ..................... 122
Zack Crouch (9) .......................... 122
Jessica Key (10) ......................... 123
Corey Edmunds (9) .................... 123
Owen Case (9) ............................ 124
Tom English (9) .......................... 124
Sarah Wren (8) ........................... 125
Elizabeth Curcillo (9) .................. 125
Rosie Huang (8) .......................... 126
Thomas Mason (9) ..................... 126
Connor Wells (8) ......................... 127
Dhaanish Mishal (8) ................... 127
Alex Grimes (8) ........................... 127
Rudi Stevens (9) ......................... 128
Isaac Shipp (8) ........................... 128

## Wicklewood Primary School, Wicklewood
Ellie Florence (7) ........................ 128
Finn Rigney (8) ........................... 129
Phoebe Cohen (8) ...................... 129
Bryony King (7) ........................... 129
Leonie Read (8) .......................... 130
Charlotte Cooper (9) .................. 130
Minnie Michlmayr (7) .................. 130
Emily Sully (8) ............................. 131
Rowan Holloway (8) ................... 131
Hamish Jeffery (7) ...................... 131
Jenson Holloway (7) ................... 132
Libby Lambert (8) ....................... 132
James Vincent (7) ...................... 132

Louise Goodings (7) ............................... 133
Hannah Spratling (7) ............................. 133
**Wilby CE (VC) Primary School, Wilby**
Katie Rodwell (7) .................................... 133
William Haigh (8) .................................... 134
Sam Morris (9) ........................................ 134
Tomas Earl (9) ........................................ 135
Louis Strehlow (8) ................................... 135
Isla Whittle (8) ........................................ 136
Shannon Curtis (9) ................................. 136
Liam Irvine (8) ........................................ 137
Alice Evans-Hendrick (9) ........................ 137
Lewis Roughton (7) ................................ 138
Jessie Evans-Hendrick (8) ..................... 138
Arwen Maguire (7) .................................. 139
Alice Wiseman (8) .................................. 139
Jasmine Irvine (8) ................................... 140
Alice Mills (8) .......................................... 140
Eddie Shearman (8) ............................... 141
Xander Redgrave (9) .............................. 141
Abbie Hawes (9) ..................................... 142
Henry Bishop (7) ..................................... 142
Emily Bullock (9) ..................................... 143
Lily Strehlow (8) ...................................... 143
James Balls (7) ....................................... 143

# The Poems

## Recipe For A Perfect Family

1. To begin with add a loving mum
2. A bag of love
3. 1 Russian Blue
4. Stir till blue and hairy
5. Then add a 10-year-old boy
6. A 7-year-old girl
7. Stir till creamy and light
8. Last of all add a dad.

Bake for an hour
Serve with 2 cars and a house.

**Joshua Wilkins (10)**
**Bramfield House School, Bramfield**

## Recipe Poem

Begin with a bag full of love
This will make the mixture creamy
Add a teaspoon of happiness
And an ounce of kindness
Mix with carnivals.

**Ethan Baker (11)**
**Bramfield House School, Bramfield**

## I Saw A Penguin

I saw a penguin swallow a big humpback whale.
I saw a lion jump like a kangaroo.
I saw a snake slither through a wall.
I saw a spider clutter and crash through my brain.
I saw a shark flying like a humpback whale in mid-air.
I saw a fish walk under a lorry.
I saw a crab run around the world.
I saw a pig run a marathon.
I saw an ostrich roll in the mud.
I saw an owl fly into a wall going *bong!*
I saw a foot come to life.
I saw a tree walk over a house.
I saw a piece of paper get a cut.

**Harry Wright (9)**
**Foulsham Primary School, Foulsham**

## The Girl With The Brown Satchel

One sunny day a girl was born,
She had eyes as blue as azure
And a beautiful smile.
People melted with joy when she laughed.
Even in the bleak, white hospital,
She made it bright
With every smile she smiled.

One sunny day a girl turned three
And there was a huge party.
Aunties and uncles and granny too
All came to her house.
She got given a brown satchel
And loved it so much
That when the cake came out,
She wished she'd never lose it!

One sunny and snowy day a girl woke
To presents under a tree.
She squealed with delight
As she uncovered a brand new bike.
She rode it day after day
To the shops and then Granny's
And finally, back home again.

One sunny day a girl tried to ride her bike
Without the stabilisers.
She fell and fell and fell some more,
Until she finally cracked it.
To celebrate, she bought some chocolate
With money from her satchel
And never forgot that day!

One sunny day a girl went to the pool,
(On her bike of course!)
And her father taught her to swim.
She splished and sploshed
And splashed a bit too,
And soon,
She could swim like a fish!

One sunny day a girl tried to climb a tree.
Her footing slipped and she landed
With a *thump* on her arm.
An ambulance came

And took her away and her arm
Was in a cast for weeks!
But soon after
She was climbing the tree again!

One sunny day a girl wouldn't let go
Of her mum's hand.
It was her first day at school
And she was petrified.
She had her brown satchel
And rode there on her bike.
Even though she was scared,
She loved it the minute she let go
Of her mum's hand.
She loved art and the years flew by
Like minutes.

One sunny day a girl got on the school bus
To her first day at high school.
It was huge at first.
She got lost a few times,
But soon she was walking round like a pro!
She carried her brown satchel everywhere,
Even though it was now worn and scuffed
And she was soon going to study art
At college.

**Saffron Hedges (10)**
**Foulsham Primary School, Foulsham**

## The Test

Here I am sitting in class.
All I can hear is *boom, boom, blast!*
I hate the sound of it all.
I wish I was in a paddling pool.
We're doing a test.
I'm going to do my best.
At last I did it.
I'm so proud of myself.
I'm now going home singing.
Hip, hip, hooray.

**Millie Notley (10)**
**Foulsham Primary School, Foulsham**

## As Special As Pearls

The warm, crystal-clear water tickled my skin
As I darted around happily.
The fish were as bright as the sun,
The coral was as colourful as a rainbow.
The slimy seaweed is the best toy for the cheeky dolphins
And they throw it up playfully.
But then, what's that?
A string of pearls shining delicately.
I picked it up and put it on.
At once I felt so strange,
Then a tail appeared, such a beautiful tail,
I have never felt such a thing.
I grin and dive here and there,
Laughing all the time.
But then, oh no, I've swum too far now.
I am small and lost.
Big fish are circling me,
Baring their teeth hungrily.
I scream and shout but nothing changes.
I swish my tail once more,
Then the fierce fish leap at me . . .

Then I wake, scared and sweating
In my cosy bed.
I sigh and walk over to my window.
I watch the rough, tough sea
Crash against the smooth, slimy rocks.
I sigh once more, a sad sigh.
I do so wish I could swim like a fish,
I do so wish I was not afraid.
I wish and wish I was allowed out there
With all my friends and family,
But I know I have to go now,
I know it is time to fulfil my dreams
And learn to swim,
To stop dreaming night and day.
There are no sharks out there,
I don't know why I shake with fear
Each time I'm in the bath.
Don't ask me how I know
Because a little fish told me.
Yes, a very, very little fish indeed.
So thank you, fish, oh little fish

Thank you so, so much.
For now I know I am able to swim as quick as a fish,
So fish bye-bye, now I am going swimming.
So now I say don't give up,
Never forget fate,
Because not everyone has a fish like mine.

**Abigail Cater (10)**
**Foulsham Primary School, Foulsham**

## The Great Escape

Bonny the Lab was sleeping like a cat,
Scruff flew in and said, 'The phone, get the phone!'
She woke and got the phone.
She spoke, 'Hello?' But no reply.
Scruff put the phone down
And said, 'Jack, that boy's always up to no good.'

They flew out into the crisp spring air,
They flew, flew, flew for what felt like hours,
Over the house and over the trees.
They arrived at Jack's very special secret lab.

They hid behind a lab table.
George saw the tip of Scruff's tail.
He got the axe,
He swung, he missed.
Bonny said, 'Stop!'
He stopped. He was a statue for a while.
He turned to look and started to run.
He made her walk back.
Nowhere to run, nowhere to hide,
So all she could do was fly.
She grabbed Scruff and found a window.
She'd never actually gone through a window.
They'd gone home, no harm done.
Bonny was worn out, she went back to sleep.
Scruff flew out and didn't make a peep.

**Mae Betts (10)**
**Foulsham Primary School, Foulsham**

## Trapped!

A slippery, slimy snake
Slithers through the wood,
The snake spots a bird as bright as a light
And says, 'That looks good!'
The snake was an elephant as he gobbled
And he chewed and swallowed it whole.
Then he saw a juicy, tasty, hairy mole.
A slippery, slimy snake
Spotted a giraffe, he thought it was funny.
He started to laugh.
He suddenly thought,
*I'm not eating that,*
*It's far too fat.*
A slippery, slimy snake
Saw something brown.
He slithered towards
And began to frown.
Suddenly, all went black.
He found he was in a back-pack.
Night and day
He slept along the way.
With a tear,
Sunlight shone upon the snake
Which gave him a fright.
But he didn't care.
A slippery, slimy snake
Wanders up and down
While on his face there is a big frown.
He watches from behind glass,
Faces walking past.
Men and boys, girls and women too,
Walking to the gift shop
To buy something new.
Finally, when the day is done,
People leaving and coming for more fun.
The gates went *screech*
As they began to close,
The snake was happy

He didn't have to pose.
A slippery, slimy snake
Begins to shut his eyes,
Time to sleep . . .

**Callum Pell (11)**
**Foulsham Primary School, Foulsham**

## Big Bold Norwich City

Cities are big, bold and tall.
You see shops, cars, planes and all.
People are dressed smart and cool
With birds going *tweet tweet*
While eating half-eaten food.
And homeless people who you think are sad,
Are happy and cheerful for a moment of time.
Thousands of people rush through this city
To catch planes, trains and to rush through the shops
To see friends and family
In their little or large flats.

You see binmen as dirty as mouldy sloths,
Cleaning up after other people.
And policemen are dressed as smart as the Queen.

People are cheerful when eating their lunch
Or going to the shops whether they're from this country or not.
You can see lots of people in Norwich City.
The man who mimes to music,
The old, funny sort
With the big, bulgy puppet
That wiggles and wiggles like mad.
Norwich City is a great, great place,
But it is the end of the day
And just about everyone has gone away.

**Hollie Godfrey (11)**
**Foulsham Primary School, Foulsham**

## The Atlantic Ocean

The ocean waves were coming in
Tommy the dolphin was jumping
In and out of the waves.
*Splash!*

Julie the squid was having tea
In her rock house.
*Clang, clang!*

Victoria was in the ocean
On her surfboard.
*Splash!*
Victoria fell off the surfboard.

The water was freezing cold
Tommy the dolphin came to Victoria
Victoria got on Tommy's back
Tommy took Victoria to the sand.

Pincers the crab
Was looking for food to eat.

Jodie the shark was swimming
In the ocean.
*Splash!*
Pincers the crab found a dead fish to eat
*Chump! Chump!*

Then Victoria's friends came
To go surfing with her in the ocean.
After an hour
They came back to the sand.
Victoria fell over a big rock.
*Bang! Crash! Wallop! Ouch!*

Then Victoria's friends
Came running to Victoria,
'Are you OK?'
'Not really.'

Then Tommy the dolphin
Came up to everyone on the sand.

**Danielle Nabarro (9)**
**Foulsham Primary School, Foulsham**

## A Day At The Stable

A day at the stables
What can be better?
An ice cream or chocolate maybe
But for some of us it's a perfect day.

Now the day has started
We get ready for the day ahead
We got dressed and had breakfast
And made lunch.

We all rushed to the stable
To feed the horses
And make them ready for the busy day
A little groom and they were ready.

The riders arrived
And got ready
Groomed the horses properly
Tacked them up for the hack and rode off with a smile.

They saw a peacock
A colourful one
And a butterfly as quick as a fairy
And an ant, well lots of them.

They were riding down the road
*Clip-clop, clip-clop*
Down the road they went
*Clip-clop, clip-clop*

The horses' legs moved like a human
The trees cracked their arms in the strong wind
They galloped down the road as fast as they could
*Clip-clop, clip-clop,* round the corner out of sight.

They reached the picnic site
They had a lovely time
But they didn't want to go

They took two hours to get back
Then took one hour to untack
Then it was time to go.

**Abbie Watts (9)**
**Foulsham Primary School, Foulsham**

## Mr Orange

The fruit bowl was sitting on the crystal-white worktop.
Bananas as yellow as the midday sun.
Apples as green as the summer grass.
Nothing out of the ordinary?
Apart from Mr Orange!

Mr Orange rolled on the crystal-white worktop,
Not knowing a cat was surging beneath him.
The cat jumped like a fast frisbee
And drifted along the worktop at a steady speed.

Mr Orange jumped out of his orange peel skin,
He rolled as fast as a V8 engine under his orange skin.
He rolled down the handle of the broom,
Flying like a red arrow, but orange.

He rushed out of the kitchen like a fly on fire,
Like rubber orange, he squeezed through the letterbox.
There, standing before him was the orange tree,
His eyes grew huge like lollipops.

He started rolling,
Turning, he started to tear up the lawn.
He rushed up the trunk, as brown as sludgy mud
And there he was, back where he had been and belonged.

**Sam Bush (10)**
**Foulsham Primary School, Foulsham**

## The Budgie

The budgie, a colourful bird,
The budgie, a brightly coloured bird,
Cheeky and it's not the quietest,
The budgie, an ear-shattering bird,
Causing much dust and eating much food.
The budgie originates from Australia.
The budgie, sometimes kind and sometimes not,
The budgie is usually warm and feels like silky-soft cotton wool.
Budgies, truly wonderful birds,
Kind, noisy and it warms me inside.

**Max Wright (11)**
**Foulsham Primary School, Foulsham**

## The Thieves

In a small town there was some gold.
People liked the gold.
It was as sparkly as the stars.
In the morning some people came.
They were on horses as tall as a table.
They had horrible, rotten teeth.
They tried to steal the gold,
But we were as angry as monkeys
When you steal their fruit.
We fought them off and stole the gold back
As fast as a flash.
We don't let anyone steal our gold.
They came back.
We won, so go away.
They were as sad as a baby
When it drops its ice cream
Because they did not get the gold.
They rode away on their horses.
They were so desperate
For the outstanding gold.
They loved it.

**Jordan Day (10)**
**Foulsham Primary School, Foulsham**

## Wiz Ping Pong

On the Wiz Ping Pong
Where the cows go bong
And all the monkeys *boo!*

I once saw a fox who was with an ox
At the bottom of a pool.
There the children waiting to see the spotted giraffe
Who was sitting at the bottom of the sea.

The children were waiting for the keeper to open the gate
To see what they could see.
They might see the dog who talks like a frog,
They might see the lion creeping around

At the Wiz Ping Pong zoo!

**Bethan Levesley (9)**
**Foulsham Primary School, Foulsham**

## The Chop!

I was woken by my father,
His early morning call.
I know I must get up and dressed
For duty forever calls,
But if my master nags me
And harries me through the day,
Who will be there to comfort me
When my father goes away?

Off my father's head will go,
I mourn his loss with two sharp blows.
The axe like a snarling dog,
My father ready for *the chop!*
*Bang, bang!* On the wooden block,
*Bang, bang!* To finish him off.

Oh, how I try to get through the day,
I cry myself to sleep in a way.
I wake up and life is so not fair,
Everyone knows everyone's been there.
Loss of lovers, leaps and bounds,
You to mourn their loss without a sound.

**Anna Sinclair (10)**
**Foulsham Primary School, Foulsham**

## Creeped Out!

There I was inside, only because the door was open wide,
I saw a red velvet carpet looping the stairs,
I walked to the window and saw a ghost.
*Woo, wuu, woo, wuu!* I heard the ghost say.
Its eyes, like a human's, looked into mine.
I was terrified.
My hair spiked up like a hedgehog,
My jaw dropped wide.
A musty smell greeted me while bats filled the sky.
They were squealing and squawking like wild things.
All the time I felt like somebody was watching over my shoulder,
Watching every step and move.
Suddenly, I saw the ghost do the groove!
I was shocked. I ran to the stairs and ran my finger up the barrier.
I slowly walked up.
I saw a door in front, I touched the handle, made of gold.
I have to say it was very cold.
I took a deep breath and opened the door.
I walked inside and . . . *bang!*
'Oww!' I bumped my head.

**Abigail Burnham (11)**
**Foulsham Primary School, Foulsham**

## Paradise Island

Here I sit and what can I see?
The big, gold sun gleaming over the beautiful sea.
The tall, green palm trees are like giants swaying in the breeze
And the sea gleaming beautifully in the daylight.
I can see a big fat pool as it waits for me!

Here I sit and what can I hear?
The waves going *whoosh!* as they hit the cracking wall,
The Spanish band playing their amazing music
And the chatting of all the lovely people.

Here I sit and what can I smell?
The scrumptious, sizzling food, sizzling away,
But there is a smell that doesn't smell so good,
The salty sea water that gets in your mouth.

Here I sit and what can I feel?
The boiling sun like a frying pan touching my burnt skin.
As I sit here alone, I think to myself,
*This beach is like a very strong man,*
But I wish that you were here with me!

**Abbie Claxton (11)**
**Foulsham Primary School, Foulsham**

## Callum And The Crab!

There he was, Callum travelling to the beach.
He was going in his Nissan Cube.
He could only just see the neon green sea.
It was pounding over the pink sand dunes.
The sand was slowly swept away by the sea,
It was as pink as candyfloss.
The sea slithered across the sand.
The sea was as green as summer grass
And as bright as the sun.
*Splash, splash!* went the sea in the background.
He rolled down the sand dune and sat up.
He shouted, 'Ouch!' and jumped up.
There was a crab underneath him.
The crab said, 'Sorry, you were squishing me.'
'Sorry. I was having fun. Can we be friends?' said Callum.
Crab said, 'Yes, OK then.'
They both shouted, 'Yay!'
So they got the radio and had a party.
Then they took Crab home and he was their pet.

**Callum Bowen-Jones (10)**
**Foulsham Primary School, Foulsham**

## Inside My Fridge!

Inside my fridge there is lots to eat for every different day of the week:
Bacon, broccoli, bananas too, scrumptious food for all of you.
But what really happens inside my fridge no one can ever tell.
For in my fridge the food is alive and boy, does it smell.
I will introduce you to all of my mates, sorry they are a bit late.
Now we have Bob the bristly broccoli,
Callum the crazy carrot,
Tom the Turkish tomato,
Abigail the amazing apple,
Pat the perfect potato,
Max the mouldy milk and
James the jumpy juice.
My fridge is as bright as the sun and weighs a ton.
*Slam!* shut the fridge before they get warm and run out in a swarm.
This is my fridge and these are my friends,
I'm sorry but this is where our story ends.
I know we'll meet again someday,
So let's shake hands and say hooray.

**Lexie Cox (11)**
**Foulsham Primary School, Foulsham**

## Trenches

The rain poured down in a relentless wave,
It was like a freezing knife cutting at our faces.
It poured and poured and pounded
On the duckboards.
We were waiting, waiting for the very shot
That was going to start the fire fight.
A bellowing shout came from the German trench,
*Bang!* And all hell broke loose!

The thundering blows of our Lebel rifles
And the crackling noise of the Maxim machine-guns,
Also groans of dying men.
I crawled out of the safety of the trench . . .
Then I realised I was stuck on the barbed wire.
Squirming like a worm, like a pig in the mud,
I could hear the gunshots getting closer and closer,
Until I felt the one that finished me off!

**Finlay Bond (11)**
**Foulsham Primary School, Foulsham**

## In The Woods

In the cold, snowing wood
In a rickety, old, big house
Lives a man called Tom
With his trusty shotgun.

He heard a *bang!*
He runs outside
On the ground is something grey
It's a rabbit, a small, fluffy rabbit.

Its eyes are staring
Its nose as big as a golf ball
Its legs are as small as a pen
It must be dead.

Tom picks up the rabbit
Tom takes it in the house
He won't be hungry tonight
Rabbit stew for tea!

**Reece Nabarro (11)**
**Foulsham Primary School, Foulsham**

## John And His Dog

There was a man called John
Who was taking his dog for a walk.
They were walking at the city park.
John had a very big nose
But he was so very kind.
'Cause at the time it was winter,
He was dressed in so, so many layers.
'Cause the snow was very deep,
He had wellies up to the knee.
His dog had a brown, fluffy coat,
As fluffy as a blanket.
The snow was a white blanket
Over the grassy floor.
The snow was white, white, white,
The snow was white as white could be.
The dog was barking and John was tired,
So what they did was set off home.

**Finley Castell (10)**
**Foulsham Primary School, Foulsham**

## The Flying Car Adventure

The magic car, it flies high in the sky,
Seeing the Northern Lights,
The colours are purple, blue, yellow,
Green, red and pink.

The flying car saw a huge, silver castle,
The flying car saw a huge, silver castle,
A huge red, blue and black dragon
Flew in front of the flying car.

It had red flames coming out of its mouth
And the red flames were as red as lava.
The dragon shot out red flames at the flying car.
The flying car magically got a shield and guns out.

The flying car shot the dragon with its guns and went *bang!*
The dragon fell down dead.
The flying car flew safely to the silver castle.

**Dylan Hann (10)**
**Foulsham Primary School, Foulsham**

## I Saw A Monkey Fly

I saw a monkey fly
I saw a monkey fly high
I saw a monkey eat a fly
I saw a monkey ride a butterfly

I saw a pig playing on the Wii
I saw a pig fighting a bee
I saw a pig jump down a tree

I saw a caterpillar riding a bike
I saw a caterpillar go on a hike
I saw a caterpillar get eaten by a pike
I saw a caterpillar and his name was Mike

I saw a kangaroo walk down the street
I saw a kangaroo eat a sweet
I saw a kangaroo who doesn't like meat
I saw a kangaroo thumping a beat with his feet.

**Megan Hales (10)**
**Foulsham Primary School, Foulsham**

## Dead Warriors

I saw, I saw, I saw,
A big, big castle.
I saw, I saw, I saw,
A small, small skeleton.
I saw, I saw, I saw,
A big, big skeleton army.
I heard, I heard, I heard,
The bones clatter, clatter on the old dusty road.
*Bang, bang, clatter, clatter, bang,*
*Bang, bang, clatter, clatter, bang.*
Nearer, nearer, nearer,
Louder, louder, louder it comes.
I stop, I stare, I see, I see, I see . . .
Nothing.
I wake up,
I see my bedroom.

**Austin Searjeant (9)**
**Foulsham Primary School, Foulsham**

## Scratch, Scratch, Scratch

I saw a big, big bite
Like a balloon,
On my gorgeous horse.
I wonder who did that.
I wonder.

*Scratch, scratch, scratch!*

I know it was those nasty nits,
They are so nasty.
They bite my gorgeous horse.
It's Natalie with her nasty children.
They also bit me all day long.
They bite my gorgeous skin
And it hurts me all day long.
I go, 'Ouch! Ouch! Ouch! Ouch!'
All day long.

**Abbie Colman (10)**
**Foulsham Primary School, Foulsham**

# Months

Months, months all over the world
January, February and more

January all cold, January all shivery
Wrap up warm

February like January, sometimes raining
Sometimes snowing

March is windy, sometimes sunny
Snowdrops rising

April showers, daffodils bowing
Umbrellas up

May sunshine, lukewarm
Trees are budding

June, getting ready for summer
Leaves appearing

July hot, lazy summer days
Having fun on the beach

August sunshine, flowers grow
Children playing in the park

September leaves turning golden
Cooling down

October, leaves fall, Halloween time
Children trick or treating

November cold days, colder nights
Fireworks and bonfires glowing

December, time to celebrate
Christmas presents, Santa's coming.

**Courtney Burton (8)**
**Great Massingham CE Primary School, Great Massingham**

## Scary Or Funny?

Falling building
Explosion went wrong
Building crashes
That went wrong.

Dreaded combine harvester
Playing kid
Suspicious noise
Shredded end.

Flying bird
Wings spread wide
Lightning strikes
Kentucky fried.

Wobbly bridge
Walk across
Planks give way
Tragic loss.

Spoiled spaniel
Overfed
One more bun
Very dead.

Winter skating
Latest fad
Thawing ice
Very sad.

High wire act
No safety net
Just how daft
Can you get?

**Troy Bolt (10)**
**Great Massingham CE Primary School, Great Massingham**

## Disasters

Charging bull.
Open gate.
What's that noise?
Oops! Too late.

Flying bird.
Strikes lightning.
Very sad.
It's almost frightening.

Girl on bike.
Trailing skirt.
Broken wheel.
Very hurt.

Playful dog.
Near a road.
Cars come by.
End of the road.

Falling building.
Explosion went wrong.
Building crashes.
Very wrong.

**Charlie Reeve (9)**
**Great Massingham CE Primary School, Great Massingham**

## Angels

When we see a snow-white feather resting on the ground
That's a sign that our angels are around.
Although we may not see them and they don't make a sound
Whenever they are needed our angel is around.
A guardian angel walks with us, sent from above
Their lovely wings surround us and enfold us with love.
Trust in your guardian angel and you will surely find that you feel loved
And protected and will have peace of mind.
There is a guardian angel who's by your side
Who will help in life's decisions if you let her be your guide.
If you choose to believe you'll soon have confirmation
That angels do exist for you'll be filled with inspiration.

**Nicholas Stanley (10)**
**Great Massingham CE Primary School, Great Massingham**

## The Dragon

In a big, big cave, inside the desert,
Nothing lives there, not a ferret.
But something does, something weird,
Something large, something feared!

With dark red eyes, light green scales,
Colossal wings and two tails,
Very sharp spines, razor-sharp claws,
Blade-like teeth, massive paws.

Something stirred it, bad mistake,
It opened its eye, it's awake!
Raised its head, extended its legs,
This massive beast, don't eat eggs!

The huge beast, broke through the wall,
Jumping high, scales and all.
Spreading its wings, like a massive kite,
With long, long tails and a strong *bite*.

Then it flew into the distance, never to be seen again,
Not in sun, not in snow, not even in the rain.
No one knows where it is now, although some people say they do,
Because all the swamps in the world are created by its poo!

**Adam Clarke (11)**
**Great Massingham CE Primary School, Great Massingham**

## What I Saw

I saw a horse in the wood
I thought I'd catch it if I could
I could not see the horse's head
But I still followed where it led

I knew it was a horse, I saw its tail
I tried to follow it down the trail
It was a horse I could have sworn
I could not believe my eyes
It was a unicorn!

**Lucy Barlow (9)**
**Great Massingham CE Primary School, Great Massingham**

## I Love Maths

Maths is fun
Maths is great
We count in tens
As we calculate

We learn our tables
We learn to subtract
We learn to divide
Just like that!

We discover shapes
We investigate fractions
Halves and quarters
There are so many actions

Maths is useful
For when we buy sweets
When we play instruments
We can count the beats

I love maths
I think it's great
I think it's fun
I love to calculate.

**Conner Curson (8)**
**Great Massingham CE Primary School, Great Massingham**

## The Naughty Dragon

There was a dragon called Jay
Who loved to mess around in the hay
He was always being naughty
Every dragon called him Shorty

He was always breathing fire
And was always being admired
He broke many precious things
And upset his little siblings.

**Tigga Aldiss (8)**
**Great Massingham CE Primary School, Great Massingham**

## Sweeties!

Sweeties, sweeties, in the store!
Sweeties, sweeties, chocolates galore!

Lollipops, lollipops,
Bop, pop, bop!

Ice cream, ice cream,
On the telly screen!

Chocolate, chocolate, stuff them in!
I can't believe people can throw it in the bin!

Chocolate sprinkles, rainbow sprinkles,
Strawberry sprinkles!

Sprinkles, I love, I love them all!
Come on everyone! Off to the sweet stall.

**Bethany Gibson-Hill (11)**
Great Massingham CE Primary School, Great Massingham

## Halloween

At Halloween it all comes around
At Halloween the hounds howl
They lurk by gravestones ready to pounce
While children stuff sweets and say trick or treat
Treat means happiness for all
Trick means darkness, watch a smile fall
Costumes, costumes, costumes galore
Look, there's a bat, there's a boar
There are more costumes, of course, every sort
But maybe not a horse
When it's all over you're snug at home
With a witch at the window and a ghost in your bed
You can't get Halloween out of your head.

**Kimberley Cooper (10)**
Great Massingham CE Primary School, Great Massingham

## I Like Skipping

I like skipping left and right
I like skipping day and night
I like skipping with my friends
I like skipping round the bend

I like skipping like crazy
I like skipping in the daisies
I like skipping on the deck
I like skipping around the wreck.

**Ellie Overson (7)**
Great Massingham CE Primary School, Great Massingham

## Side Stepping

I like side stepping left to right
I like side stepping day and night
I like side stepping with my friends
I like side stepping on the Fens

Side stepping makes you hot
I like side stepping on the spot
I like side stepping in the daffodils
I like side stepping in the fields.

**Louise Clarke (7)**
Great Massingham CE Primary School, Great Massingham

## Life

Life is about you
Life is about me
Life is about everyone
Life is about animals and species
Life is about the creation of the world
Life is about food and drink
Life is about everything on the Earth.

**Luke Fryett (10)**
Great Massingham CE Primary School, Great Massingham

## Winter

Winter is soft as snow.
Winter is cold as ice.
Winter is sharp as an icicle.
Winter smells like an apple.
Winter feels like ice cream.
Winter is so luscious as you lay in it.

**Chloe Harper (9)**
**Great Massingham CE Primary School, Great Massingham**

## TV

TV is fun, sometimes you *scream*
It's funny, just like me
TV is nice and sweet
It can make you cry!
Oh yes, do you need a tissue?

**Maisie Bale (8)**
**Hainford Primary Partnership School, Hainford**

## The Highwayman
*(Based on 'The Highwayman' by Alfred Noyes)*

The highwayman came riding,
Through the cloudy fog,
He rides on a horse
And carries a pistol,
Walking his faithful dog.

Whipping the shutters
To lock and bolt,
He hears a creaking noise,
Sees the ostler walking around,
So he tells the horse to halt.

The highwayman came riding,
Through the cloudy fog,
A ghostly figure,
That's what you will see,
With his mystical dog.

**Olivia Hill (9)**
**Hainford Primary Partnership School, Hainford**

## The Highwayman
*(Inspired by 'The Highwayman' by Alfred Noyes)*

The highwayman is ready for action
After his black-eyed daughter died
He ran towards the men
And he got his sword out
And ran towards the men
A bullet struck his head
Soon there was blood everywhere
His ghost came out of his body
So every night
If you hear a creak
It is him.

**Bradley Constable (8)**
**Hainford Primary Partnership School, Hainford**

## Farming

A ll my crops are growing
G rowing like you've never seen before
R eaping them in
I nto the barn it goes
C rops of wheat
U nder the dryer
L ovely to make bread to eat
T oast for breakfast
U dders getting milk from the cow
R eady to drink
E arly in the morning.

**Adam Sarsby (9)**
**Hainford Primary Partnership School, Hainford**

## Fishing

Going to the lake with Mike to catch a pike
Mike had to pull on the rod while someone caught cod.
We threw a float in to find out we'd caught a boat.
The float went under, but suddenly, there was thunder,
So he went home beginning to groan.

**Joseph Veriod (9)**
**Hainford Primary Partnership School, Hainford**

## Farm Animals

Horses are big and
Ready to be ridden
Cows are to be milked
Chickens are there to give us eggs.

Horses can jump as high as Big Ben
Cows are as strong as an elephant
Chickens are as red as highland cattle.

Horses run in the wind
Cows munch away
Chickens peck with their bums held high.

**Matthew Germany (10)**
**Hainford Primary Partnership School, Hainford**

## Winter

Looking outside the window this morning
And all you could see was fluffy white stuff
Down below your feet.
You see little children playing on the front lawn,
They must be cold out there,
But you are nice and warm!
Now getting ready to go outside,
Opening the door there is a big gust of wind.
Then you decide you don't want to go outside any more.

**Chloe McMullon (8)**
**Hainford Primary Partnership School, Hainford**

## My Fish

This little fish of mine
White and black
Stripes on his back
And his name's Jack.

He swims in the bath
He swims in the sink
He swims in his fish tank
What do you think?

**Leestefan Drake (10)**
**Hainford Primary Partnership School, Hainford**

## Friends

There are so many friends,
You can have best friends,
You can also have friends
That live far away from you.

You can have funny friends
And weird friends as well.
You can have kind and helpful friends
And some that are great.

**Lily Bates (8)**
**Hainford Primary Partnership School, Hainford**

## The Highway Horse

Trudging along the dusty road,
Stumbling beneath my back-breaking load.
Tripping through curling fingers of mist,
Constantly hit by my master's fist.
Limping up to the old inn door,
My master jumps off, a relief from saddle sore.
Standing outside the rickety inn,
The penetrating cold a terrible sin.

**Helena Mellows (9)**
**Hainford Primary Partnership School, Hainford**

## Football

F riends like to play football with you
O ff the pitch if you are red carded
O ff the pitch you are injured
T ick-tock, the time is nearly half-time
B all through for Pelé, what a goal!
A crobatic Pelé jumping with joy
L eft foot shot like Messi, what a miss
L ionel Messi scores and the score is 1-1, full time.

**Scott Harwood (8)**
**Hainford Primary Partnership School, Hainford**

## The Sky

The sky is so fun
You will never know what will happen
You will never know
When it will snow
Because it is the weather
Sometimes the sky is so dull
But I don't mind
It will be sunny one day.

**Ryan Watker (9)**
**Hainford Primary Partnership School, Hainford**

## Football

Football is the best
Controlling the ball on my chest
I practise my skills
Up the hills
And I also get some tips from my coach
And the ball is through to me
And I score with my right foot.

**Andrew Howes (9)**
**Hainford Primary Partnership School, Hainford**

## Victorian

Carriages going past laughing at him,
All the lights are very dim,
The floor as dirty as a wet, muddy dog,
You can see their faces as dull as a brick wall,
Trying to run away but the workhouse pulls you back in,
Forced to work all day, until your fingers are red with pain.
I am a Victorian!

**Francesca Le Mesurier (10)**
**Hainford Primary Partnership School, Hainford**

## In The City

Busy city, different shops,
Lots of cop cars zooming about,
Lots of fights late at night,
Police and bouncers have to sort it out.
Cars beeping, burglars creeping,
That's what goes on in the city.

**Georgia Stannett (9)**
**Hainford Primary Partnership School, Hainford**

## Space

S pace you can jump
P utting my burning hand on the sun
A ir is swirling around me
C alling for help
E ven though the sun is lava
   I'm OK.

**Cole Snowling-Dunford (8)**
**Hainford Primary Partnership School, Hainford**

## Spring

As the wind blows and flowers blossom,
Bunnies jump around in the long, green grass.
The tree branches swish side by side
And the birds land somewhere nearby.

**Ellen Baker-Breame (9)**
**Hainford Primary Partnership School, Hainford**

## The Xbox

The sky was dull
And a little boy was playing on an Xbox
His brother couldn't see him
But he could hear his game!

**James Lord (9)**
**Hainford Primary Partnership School, Hainford**

## Roses Are Red

This is my rhyme
It won't take much time

Roses are red, violets are blue
Did you know, I really love you?

Roses are red, violets are blue
Love never crossed my mind until I met you!

That was my rhyme
It didn't take much time.

**Chloe Sparks (8)**
**Hardwick Primary School, Bury St Edmunds**

## Feelings About You

When you're blue,
I still love you

When you're glum,
Call your mum

When you're snappy,
Please be happy

When you're sad,
Don't be bad.

**Ellie Parker (8)**
**Hardwick Primary School, Bury St Edmunds**

## A Perfect Garden

A perfect garden would have a dark green lawn
Sprinkled with autumn leaves
A perfect garden would have a white and grey stony path
Near the trees
A perfect garden would have a sparkling blue river
Gushing slowly by the fence
A perfect garden would always have a bench!

**Benjamin Foreman (9)**
**Hardwick Primary School, Bury St Edmunds**

## My Monsters And The Imaginary World

My monster is Fang,
When he heard a bang,
He blamed it on Tango.
Tango likes mango,
He is my other monster.
Other monsters call him Pongster,
Because he smells.
He just now yelled,
I'd better go,
Ow! My toe!
My monster lives in a house
With a chocolate pool,
Everyone thinks it's cool.
It has marshmallow floaties
And candyfloss boaties.
They live in trees,
Trees that don't need keys,
And trees that grow yummy food.
Oh great, Fang is in a mood
And that's my imaginary world!

**Maisie Robinson (8)**
**Hevingham Primary School, Hevingham**

## My Monster

My monster has prickles,
But eats pickles,
She has a green bow,
Her dad works in the tow,
Her dad is called Kim,
He goes to the gym.

My monster has prickles,
But eats pickles,
She is purple,
When she's mad she ripples,
She lives above a river,
Her favourite dinner is liver
And that's my monster.

**Libby Field (9)**
**Hevingham Primary School, Hevingham**

## My World

In my world the ice cream palace is as cold as can be,
The flying saucers are as sweet as chocolate bars,
While the royal castle is as red as roses
With the hot chocolate cage like sweets
Meanwhile the toffee lake island as soft as velvet.

The chocolate sea as lovely as Heaven,
Then the toffee lake like melted fudge,
Next the chocolate riverboats as dark as 70% cocoa,
With the raining sweet cloud as hard as a tree
And finally, the Vienetta island as scrumdiddlyumptious
As an invented sweet!

**Olivia Bullen (8)**
**Hevingham Primary School, Hevingham**

## Gum Gum B

My monster has hair like soft bear's fur,
A nose as hard as rock,
Eyes like massive gobstoppers,
Ears as squishy as Ben & Jerry's ice cream.

My monster is as tough as Iron Man,
As cool as ice,
As scary as Garfield,
As smelly as aftershave,
As sneaky as a ninja.
My monster is called Gum Gum B.

**Cameron Earnshaw (9)**
**Hevingham Primary School, Hevingham**

## My Monster

This monster is as tall as Mount Everest,
His feet are as big as a school,
Eyes like fire,
His fur feels like grass,
He roars as loud as a volcano,
He is more frightening than a zombie.

**Ethan Glynn (8)**
**Hevingham Primary School, Hevingham**

## Katsumer

My monster is called Katsumer.
His body is as fluffy as a kitten.
Teeth as sharp as knives.
Nose as red as a strawberry.
Eyes as small as a mouse.
Feet middle-sized like a school pencil pot.
Arms as short as T-rex's arms.
Ears as straight as rulers.

**Marcie Mitchell (8)**
**Hevingham Primary School, Hevingham**

## My Monster

My monster has a body like a mouldy banana,
Eyes like red lava,
A nose like a knife,
A mouth like a toothpaste tube,
Legs like long, bumpy sticks
And arms like wires.
My monster is as friendly as a dog.

**Conor Glynn (8)**
**Hevingham Primary School, Hevingham**

## Pineapple Dude

My monster has a body like a pineapple,
A mouth like a motor.
He has hair as spiky as a hedgehog.
His eyes are like gigantic luminous gobstoppers.
He has legs like a small pencil sharpener,
Arms as chubby as a baby's,
He makes a non-stop noise like a monster truck.

**Jack Ferizi (9)**
**Hevingham Primary School, Hevingham**

## Panda

This animal is as big as your thumb
He is black and white like a panda
He squeaks once a day
He has friendly eyes which twinkle
His house has everything you can think of.

**Evie Cowling (7)**
Hevingham Primary School, Hevingham

## My Monster

The boys bully Billy's brother,
The gargoyle ate Grace's grapes.
The teacher told Tilly to tickle Tommy.
The supply teacher cried in disgrace of the class
And that is my monster poem.

**Thomas Lake (7)**
Hevingham Primary School, Hevingham

## The Groovy Gorilla

The groovy gorilla glides through the jungle,
Like it's a very easy obstacle course,
Galloping on the Mediterranean,
It's the dust that annoys him.
Grasping and clinging,
Onto the vines,
Like he has done it one hundred times.
Greedy and glutinous,
When it comes to dinner time,
Slurping, chomping and crunching,
It's gone in a blink of a eye.
Gorilla is very gloomy,
When it's time for bed,
But he always knows,
There is another day ahead.

**Zack Frosdick (10)**
Horning Community Primary School, Horning

## Animals Alphabet

A wkward, ambling antelope
B ig, buzzing bee
C ute, colourful chameleon
D izzy donkey dancing
E legant, enormous elephant
F lippy, flying fish
G roaning, grumpy gorilla
H ungry, hilarious horse
I nteresting, impatient iguana
J umping, jigging jaguar
K arate kicking kangaroo
L aughing, leaping leopard
M ean monkey mixing
N oisy, naughty newt
O dd, orange octopus
P retty, pale parrot
Q uick, quiet quail
R acket rabbit racing
S haking, sad snake
T alking, trendy tadpole
U nhappy, upset unicorn
V icious, violent vole
W eak, wet weasel
X ox with a fox
Y apping yak yawning
Z ooming zebra zapping.

**Lily Brittle (10)**
**Horning Community Primary School, Horning**

## Cats

The cats cluster together
Cuddly and crying.
They crawl into the box,
Being very cheeky!
Cowardly, they clamber,
Slowly, they claw.

**Jordan Evans (10)**
**Horning Community Primary School, Horning**

## Alphabet Poem

A ward ambling antelopes
B uzzing, bouncy bee
C reepy-crawly cats
D angerous, dancing dogs
E normous, excited elephants
F at, flying fish
G igantic, great giraffes
H umungous, hungry horses
I nternational, ignoring iguanas
J umping, jolly jaguars
K icking, kind koalas
L azy, leisure lions
M ad, messy monkeys
N aughty, noisy newts
O ld-fashioned, open octopus
P atient, peaceful penguins
Q uick, quiet quetzals
R are, racing rabbits
S cared, startled sharks
T angled, teased tigers
U gly, unkind umbrella bird
V iolent, vanishing viper
W hite waving weasel
eX isted, exhilarated ox
Y apping, young yak
Z ero zoom zebra.

**Amy Crockford (11)**
**Horning Community Primary School, Horning**

## The Polar Bear

A polar bear ploughing snow across the ice,
With her cubs behind her.
The polar bear rolls into the water, *splash!*
The cubs follows. *Splash! Splash!*

**James Willoughby (8)**
**Horning Community Primary School, Horning**

## Animal Poem

A nnoyed, ambling ant
B lack, burly bear
C urling, crawling caterpillar
D aring, dozing duck
E normous, exercising elephant
F iery, flying fly
G iant, grumpy giraffe
H airy, humorous horse
I mpatient, ignored iguana
J olting, jumping jaguar
K arate kicking king cobra
L ying, limping lion
M ad, manic monkey
N aughty, nasty gnat
O ily, occupied octopus
P ale, panting possum
Q uite quarrelsome quail
R efreshed, relaxed rhino
S peedy set salamander
T railing, tracking trout
U nknown, unidentified umbrella bird
V iolent, vicious viper
W heezy, waking weasel
eX hilarated, excited ox
Y anking, yelping yak
Z igzag zooming zebra.

**George Frosdick (8)**
**Horning Community Primary School, Horning**

## Calves

A cute calling calf crawled crossly.
Cows can't, calves can.
Clapping cows called.
Clay clogged the calves' hearing.

**George Echlin-Riches (9)**
**Horning Community Primary School, Horning**

## The Miner Bird

The miner bird hoots, toots,
Clicks and picks, it walks silently,
Stopping, staring, listening for danger.
Hearing only silence,
It slips silently over to a tree and starts rooting around,
Listening for flicking beetles like its life depends on it.
Its feathers pick up, it's heard a sawing sound,
Quick as a wink running, tapping,
It vanishes just like it came.
In the distance never to be seen or heard from again.

**Jordan Hayton (10)**
**Horning Community Primary School, Horning**

## The Scaly Snake

A slithering, slimy, scaly snake
Slowly sways, left and right,
Safely searching for its prey.
It suddenly changes
From a slow snake to a speedy snake,
Springing into action,
Catching its prey,
It spreads its mouth
And swallows it whole.

**Auguste Jones (9)**
**Horning Community Primary School, Horning**

## The Snake

The snake that moves slowly slithers along the slimy path.
Over the slimy path it goes.
It slithers a bit more and spots its prey.
It slowly moves more and it jumps up.
It has got its prey.
It slithers along under the rock
And the slimy blood is washed away
From the big rock and disappears.
It goes back to its child.

**India Everett (8)**
**Horning Community Primary School, Horning**

## Space Poem

Jump like a
Jumping
Jupiter.

Swirl like
Saturn,
Swirly.

Spin like
A spinning
Sun.

Go to Venus
To see
The meanest.

Pooping
Pluto,
Popping along.

Superstars
Are so bright
In the night.

They shine
Like a
Shiny shimmer.

They are so bright
In the
Moonlight.

**Evie Salter (8)**
**Kelsale CE (VC) Primary School, Kelsale**

## The Earth

The Earth, third planet to the sun.
We keep warm by the sun.
Winter grows over us.
Black sky, frost and snow
But you can keep warm
By the fire steam
Rising in the moonlit sky.

**Maxwell Moore (8)**
**Kelsale CE (VC) Primary School, Kelsale**

## My Space Poem

Mad Mercury muddying Mars
Now it is not bright like all the stars.

Victorious Venus vaporising violence
Until there was a beautiful silence.

Epic Earth evaporating rain
And when we go down we use our brain.

Muddy Mars making Mercury mad
Mars is in trouble, Mercury has gone to get his dad.

Jumping, jiggly Jupiter bouncing everywhere,
Is it here? Is it here? Jiggly Jupiter is far and there.

Silly Saturn sliding by,
Take off then you're ready to fly.

Ultimate Uranus underwater
And did you know he has a daughter?

Nervous Neptune needing a navel,
Even though he lives in a stable.

Peter Pan Pluto saving Wendy,
Also his clothes are very trendy!

**Madeline Salter (8)**
**Kelsale CE (VC) Primary School, Kelsale**

## The Solar System

Silly Saturn skipping by
All those stars, I wonder why.
I can't go and see them,
Tell me why.
Milky madness in the Milky way,
Launch those rockets, I want to say.
Jumping Jupiter has jumped by,
Silly Saturn just waiting to fly.
Mad Mercury misses Mars
Whilst pretty Pluto sees the stars.

**Jenny Roberts (7)**
**Kelsale CE (VC) Primary School, Kelsale**

## My Remembrance Poem

The poppies as red as Mars,
Like the bloodstained battlefield.
The guns as loud as thunder
And the war is not yet over.

We are the soldiers, we are fighting for peace,
Peace as sweet as sugar,
Peace as sweet as candy
And the war is not yet over.

The army is lowering as fast as lightning,
Trench water as cold as ice,
The war is moving slower than a snail,
But the war is not yet over.

**Jamie Roberts (9)**
**Kelsale CE (VC) Primary School, Kelsale**

## Stars In The Sky

All those gleaming stars in the sky,
I can't go up there, tell me why?
Although they seem so pretty to see,
I just want to go up there with you and me.

All those bright bursts of fire rolling around,
Everyone just wishes that they could be found.
I can't go up there. Why, why, why?
All those gleaming stars in the sky.

**Grace Pelekanou (8)**
**Kelsale CE (VC) Primary School, Kelsale**

## Poem Of A Little Girl

The teddy is as soft as snow,
Her dress is soft as silk,
Her teddy is as scared as she is,
The girl didn't like the war,
Her hair is as smooth as a pillow,
The teddy is as sad as the girl,
The gas mask is as tight as a belt.

**Bradley Eagle (8)**
**Kelsale CE (VC) Primary School, Kelsale**

## Gas

Gas, gas, I see no gas!
Gas, like a crystal-clear lake.
I hear the siren,
Gas attack!
Gas!
Gas!
But she holds her teddy bear
As soft as a fluffy white cloud.

**Grace Watts (8)**
**Kelsale CE (VC) Primary School, Kelsale**

## Our Remembrance Poem

Remember, remember 11th November,
Soldiers went to war.
They died for us and fought for us.
As soldiers fought, poppies grew,
Poppies as red as blood.
Poppies are green on the stem,
Poppies make people remember the soldiers.

**Megan Enticknap**
**Kelsale CE (VC) Primary School, Kelsale**

## The War

The war started with a bang,
The soldiers went to fight the war.
Bangs like thunder from the guns and the bombs.
Bombs as black as the night sky.
Trickles of blood on the bodies of the soldiers.
The blood from the soldiers as red as the poppies in the fields
Where they fought.

**Poppy Stone (9)**
**Kelsale CE (VC) Primary School, Kelsale**

## Planets

Silly Saturn sliding by,
Take off then ready to fly.
Mad Mercury misses Mars,
Jump like jumping Jupiter star.
Nip like nipping Neptune,
Silly sun, hot and bright.
The biggest, best and full of might.

**Myah Ridgeon (8)**
**Kelsale CE (VC) Primary School, Kelsale**

## Remembrance Poem

The war started with a big bang with a big group.
As we die, we lie in Flanders fields with the poppies.
My poppy is like ruby-red blood shining so bright
And poppies are like red jewels in the field.
My poppy is like a red ruby lying in Flanders fields.
The soldiers are as brave as a poppy standing up for themselves.
The poppies are like a red ruby sitting there.

**Sophie Ross (8)**
**Kelsale CE (VC) Primary School, Kelsale**

## Our Remembrance Poem Using Similes

My poppy like fire and as red as blood.
My poppy is as red as a red ruby.
My poppy is as red as a strawberry.

The guns are as loud as thunder.
Explosions as bright as the sun.

So remember, remember the 11th of November.

**Fynley Hoyland (8)**
**Kelsale CE (VC) Primary School, Kelsale**

## Our Remembrance Poem

My poppy is like blood.
My poppy is as red as a raspberry.
The red on my poppy is blood of the soldiers.
The green on my poppy is like the soldiers' clothes.
The black on my poppy is like their hats.

**Grace Tanton Brown (7)**
**Kelsale CE (VC) Primary School, Kelsale**

## Space Poem

Naughty Neptune is like the silly moon.
Pluto is cold.
Ruby rocket roaring by, really likes to fly
Like a beautiful planet glittering by.
The night-time is scary but space is high.

**Cameron Ling (7)**
**Kelsale CE (VC) Primary School, Kelsale**

## Remembrance

Gas, gas, bad gas,
This girl is sadder
Than a tied up dog.
Gas, gas, mustard gas,
Makes your lungs explode.

**Aaron Nelhams (8)**
**Kelsale CE (VC) Primary School, Kelsale**

## Space

Shooting stars glittering above,
Calling comets, come to me.
Jupiter, make way for misty Mars.
Epic Earth is the best planet there will be.
Goodbye space, see you soon.

**Andy Ball (9)**
**Kelsale CE (VC) Primary School, Kelsale**

## Remembrance Day

Poppies are as red as blood,
Poppies are as cool as the wind,
Poppies are as bright as a sunbeam,
Poppies are for when we remember the soldiers
Who fought and died for us.

**Bethany Hall (8)**
**Kelsale CE (VC) Primary School, Kelsale**

## Out Of This World

Space is big, space is high,
Space has planets around.
Space has stars that twinkle and shine.
I wish there was a planet that I could call mine.

**Bethany Warren (8)**
**Kelsale CE (VC) Primary School, Kelsale**

## The Stars

All those shiny stars in the sky,
Oh my, oh my, I wish I could fly.
What a beautiful, beautiful sight.
I wish I was an astronaut.

**Amy Rowe (7)**
**Kelsale CE (VC) Primary School, Kelsale**

## Our Remembrance Poem Using Similes

The soldiers' hats were as hard as a rock,
Their uniforms were camouflaged like a leopard,
The guns make a bang as loud as a lion's roar,
A poppy is as beautiful as a butterfly.

**Scott Brown (7)**
**Kelsale CE (VC) Primary School, Kelsale**

## Space Poem

Pluto, Pluto, beautiful Pluto
Stars glittering in my dreams,
I wish I could fly!

**Cameron Buckle (8)**
**Kelsale CE (VC) Primary School, Kelsale**

## Beautiful Colours

Yellow is the colour
Of a new sunshine
Starting the day off.
When it's risen the
Colours are great.

Purple is the colour
Of a lavender field
In the countryside.
When the wind blows
It smells lovely
It is wonderful!

Green is the colour
Of nice green grass
Swaying
In the fields.

**Kloii Hood (10)**
**Middleton VC Primary School, Middleton**

## Sadness Is . . .

Like nobody on Earth
Life without fun.

Like a solar system with no stars
Earth with no seasons.

A face with no smile
Earth with no colour.

Like forever with no animals
Flowers with no soil.

**Shannon Tinkler (9)**
**Middleton VC Primary School, Middleton**

## The Three Éclair Bears

Once upon a time there were three bears
With a house equipped with flashy stone stairs.

One morning they went out for a walk
And Daddy Bear shouted, 'Do not talk!'

Now while they were in the wood
Outside their front door a young girl stood.

She peeped in the window and pushed open the door
And took off her shoes on the new polished floor.

She slipped right over but soon got up
On her right she saw a freshly smashed cup.

She went to the place where the éclairs stood on the table
And nearly tripped over a hidden cable.

She picked an éclair and said, 'That's too plain.'
The next one was rock hard like a tarmacked lane.

She bit the third and said, 'Mmm, that's nice.'
She was sure she heard the scurrying of mice.

Now she wanted to sit down and rest
She hated the first chair - it felt like a nest.

This next one has a score of five
'Thank goodness,' she said, 'I'm still alive.'

She thought the last one was best
She was sitting next to a large cherry chest.

She sat right down and oh my goodness
It collapsed beneath her - her dress was a mess!

She marched up the stairs and looked at each bed
She liked the one with the cover berry red.

Meanwhile outside the bears were returning
She woke up her belly was churning.

She ran down the stairs
And passed the big bears.

The bears never saw that girl again
She had a scare factor of a fiendish ten!

**Lauryn Bland (11)**
**Middleton VC Primary School, Middleton**

## Joy Is . . .

Like dancing through a rainbow,
Hot chocolate running down your throat.

Like winning a competition,
Finding a new friend.

Like a snowy Christmas,
Marshmallows in your mug.

Like dreaming of clouds,
Using a new felt pen.

Like reading a new book,
Swimming in blue water.

Like riding a horse,
Bare feet on minty green grass.

**Scarlet-Lilli Cooke (10)**
**Middleton VC Primary School, Middleton**

## Fear . . .

Like a spider crawling up your arm
The darkness of a cave.

Like a burning fire
Dying in your sleep.

Like a vampire about to bite you
Drowning in the deep blue sea.

Like a skeleton's bones rattling
A witch's horrible cackle.

Like the bleeping of an alien spaceship
The ghoul of your great uncle.

Like falling off a high cliff
A crow diving at you.

**Saffron Kirkpatrick (10)**
**Middleton VC Primary School, Middleton**

## Acrostic Postcard

P leasure Beach was very good.
L eft after an hour or more.
E veryone went on rides.
A nd we went on the log flume.
S aw the sea on some rides.
U p high in the sky.
R eally scary rides.
E xcellent!

B ought drinks and food.
E xcellent rides.
A nd
C ame
H ome!

**Benjamin Brandes (9)**
**Middleton VC Primary School, Middleton**

## Fear Is . . .

Like a door being shut on you
Feels like you're shrinking.

Like a cloud of shouting people
Hovering above you
Feels like a cage is over you.

Like somebody is watching you
Feels like your heart is exploding.

Like you're swirling around in
A black hole
Feels like you're frozen.

**Emma Brandes (10)**
**Middleton VC Primary School, Middleton**

## Additional Verse To Add Into The Lady Of Shalott
*(Inspired by 'The Lady Of Shalott' by Alfred Lord Tennyson)*

Sometimes she sees the children play
And jumping in the heaps of hay
Sometimes she hears the horses neigh
And trot up and down the river all day
But still she can't look down to Camelot
She sits and cries
As tears drip out of her green emerald eyes
She stares into the mirror's blue skies
The Lady of Shalott.

**Emily Holland (11)**
**Middleton VC Primary School, Middleton**

## Additional Verse To Add Into The Lady Of Shalott
*(Inspired by 'The Lady Of Shalott' by Alfred Lord Tennyson)*

Although she cannot take a peep
Sometimes she sees a gentle sheep
Or babies peacefully asleep
Sometimes she sees the children leap
Going down to tower'd Camelot
Sometimes she sees a maid in red
She cannot ever make her bed
The maid then off she sped
From the Lady of Shalott.

**Aaron Williamson (10)**
**Middleton VC Primary School, Middleton**

## Sadness Is . . .

Like no rainforest
Summer without birds
Like a black hole sucking
Your heart
People without any feelings
Like no sunlight
No friends to play
With.

**Matthew Daw (10)**
**Middleton VC Primary School, Middleton**

## Additional Verse To Add Into The Lady Of Shalott
*(Inspired by 'The Lady Of Shalott' by Alfred Lord Tennyson)*

Sometimes she sees butterflies here and there
Hovering about the trees of pear
Sometimes maidens waving hair
Knights riding by with flair
Trotting down to Camelot
And sometimes through the mirror's glass
She sees a carriage made of brass
The little daisies growing in the grass
The Lady of Shalott.

**Alex Florance (10)**
**Middleton VC Primary School, Middleton**

## Additional Verse To Add Into The Lady Of Shalott
*(Inspired by 'The Lady Of Shalott' by Alfred Lord Tennyson)*

Sometimes she sees cows and sheep
They are always laying down asleep
Sometimes children jump and leap
Ending up in a great big heap
On the road to Camelot
And sometimes she sees a bird in the sky
She would really love to fly
She's watching the barges going by
The Lady of Shalott.

**Jack George (10)**
**Middleton VC Primary School, Middleton**

## Colours

Blue is the colour of the sky
When it's a sunny day.

Ginger is the colour of my cats
When they're in the mud.

Green is the colour of an apple
When it's ready to pick.

**Lucy-May Whitear (9)**
**Middleton VC Primary School, Middleton**

## Additional Verse To Add Into The Lady Of Shalott
*(Inspired by 'The Lady Of Shalott' by Alfred Lord Tennyson)*

Sometimes she sees the fields of rye
And knights go riding by
Sometimes children walk by saying, 'Hi'
And sometimes birds fly high in the sky
On the way to tower'd Camelot
And sometimes she sees a horse towing a heavy barge
Sometimes fights and people shouting, 'Charge'
Sometimes she sees women very large
The Lady of Shalott.

**Harvey Rae (10)**
**Middleton VC Primary School, Middleton**

## Additional Verse To Add Into The Lady Of Shalott
*(Inspired by 'The Lady Of Shalott' by Alfred Lord Tennyson)*

Sometimes she sees a horse and cart
A child with laughter in their heart
Or sometimes a knight doing his part
A market about to start
All going down to Camelot
And sometimes a hard working reaper beams
A nearby window steams
And her mirror gleams
The Lady of Shalott.

**Harry Daw (10)**
**Middleton VC Primary School, Middleton**

## Death Is . . .

Death is the end of the world!
It is a Christmas without family
Flowers without petals
A forest without trees
The world without people
The world collapsing in on you!

**Bronte Rose (10)**
**Middleton VC Primary School, Middleton**

## Hope Is . . .

Like a war is over
Like a rocket launching into space
To land on the moon.

A butterfly spreading its wings
For the first time
Like a lovely future for you
And your child.

A newborn calling your name
Like playing a game.

**Chloe Marks (10)**
**Middleton VC Primary School, Middleton**

## Anger!

Anger is like . . .
Ripping up paper
Piercing through your heart.

Anger is like . . .
A rugby player tackling
You to the ground.

Anger is like splashing
In water on a
Rainy day.

**James Taylor (10)**
**Middleton VC Primary School, Middleton**

## Winter Cinquain

Frosty
Leaf on the grass
It is big and pointy
It has a bright colourful stalk
Icy.

**Billie Rust (11)**
**Middleton VC Primary School, Middleton**

## Colours

Green is the colour of swaying grass
    When the field is empty and the sun is hidden
        It is windy!

Red is the colour of a loose apple
    On the tree in the summer
        It's lunchtime.

Orange is the colour of the stars
    On my quilt when I go to bed
        Night night!

**Lynsey Marks (9)**
**Middleton VC Primary School, Middleton**

## Colours

Pink is the colour of new gloves for the winter
Blue is the time when it's icy-cold
White is for a fresh new snowman
It's the colour of the white sparkly snow
That's come for you.

**Hannah Evans (9)**
**Middleton VC Primary School, Middleton**

## Winter Cinquain

Jack Frost
Up in the sky
Making the snow sparkle
Putting the snow on leaves sparkling
Winter!

**Tommy Wilson (11)**
**Middleton VC Primary School, Middleton**

## Black Dog

The black dog
Jumps up and down
In the sunshine
Then it jumps off
And has its dinner.

**Sophie Bland (10)**
**Middleton VC Primary School, Middleton**

## Death Is . . .

A black horse kicking you
Piercing through your heart.
Like a member of your family dying
Running 100 miles in 5 minutes.

**Nick Peters (11)**
**Middleton VC Primary School, Middleton**

## Recipe For Making Adults Pleased

Get on train
Sit where Mum wants
Offer to go shopping with a parent.
Don't ask for anything when you are in the shop.
Offer to pack bags.
Don't moan when in your worst shop
Push buggy with bags under.
Carry bags.
Don't drag bags.
Don't argue with brother or sister.
Don't pick toy in toyshop.
Half way through comment on how nice Mum looks.
Sit nicely in café.
Ask for cheapest food or drink on menu.
Wait for train.
Unlock door.
Eat tea
Do not ask for dessert
Go to bed at 6 o'clock that night.

**Belinda Leech (10)**
**Oulton Broad Primary School, Oulton Broad**

## Eldorado
*(Based on 'Eldorado' by Edgar Allan Poe)*

In the mountain's heart
My journey I start,
Cold and dark.
Travelling so far
Towards the northern star
In search of Eldorado.

But on my journey
My horse Berny
Starts growing old and shivery.
I continue my trip
With an ice-blue lip
Oh, where is my Eldorado?

And as my strength
Failed me at length
I met a magnificent beast.
It helped me on my way
But I wanted to stay -
I needed to find my Eldorado.

Hallelujah we're there
Now I really do care
That all my work has paid off.
In a lovely place
The dolphins have grace
I love my Eldorado.

**Beth Scarlett (10)**
**Oulton Broad Primary School, Oulton Broad**

## I Wonder Why

I wonder why a goat can fly
I wonder why a frog jumps high
I wonder why a duck can quack
I wonder why a deer can snack
I wonder why tigers can roar
I wonder why a pig can snore
I wonder if the world will stop
Before my mum pops to the shop!

**Hope Reynolds (7)**
**Oulton Broad Primary School, Oulton Broad**

## Eldorado
*(Based on 'Eldorado' by Edgar Allan Poe)*

My journey I start,
In the village heart
Everyone's in my way
No matter what weather
I'll travel forever,
As I search for Eldorado.

My horse and me,
Must find the key,
To unlock the next chapter,
For if we don't,
My horse and me won't
Find my Eldorado.

Suddenly I see
Someone like me,
A man no older than thirty,
I ask him, 'Please do a good deed
The truth I need,
Do you know of Eldorado?'

He tells me the way,
I shout, 'Hooray!'
My journey I start again.
Suddenly I glance,
I jump and prance,
Over there, I see it,
It's my Eldorado.

**Taylor Dyer-Jackman (10)**
**Oulton Broad Primary School, Oulton Broad**

## My Eldorado Poem
*(Based on 'Eldorado' by Edgar Allan Poe)*

I raised my head from the pillow-like sand,
I brushed my poor and weakened hand,
The sand is gold and silver,
All the plants have died or withered,
By ship I was delivered,
To search for Eldorado.

In that desolate land,
I needed a helping hand,
For the days were long,
And the sun was so bright,
And so cold was the night,
That I was losing my might,
In my search for Eldorado.

No Eldorado is what I learned,
But as I swiftly turned,
A ghoulish figure beyond me fled through me,
And up I glowed,
And again my blood flowed,
And so I said, 'Where is Eldorado?'

'Eldorado you seek?
But you are too weak,
But instructions I do give,
To the end of the sand,
There is the land,
The land of Eldorado!'

**Rebecca Mawer (9)**
**Oulton Broad Primary School, Oulton Broad**

## Eldorado
*(Based on 'Eldorado' by Edgar Allan Poe)*

At the jungle's side
Me, I start to ride,
Through the dark trees
Travelling so long
Thinking of a song
In my search for Eldorado.

Travelled so long
Can't think of a song,
Down the creepy, dark forest
I'm so bold.
I'm certainly told
On my hunt for Eldorado.

On my journey I met a horse
Ride on it? Of course,
Over the mountain
Down so far
Looking for that star
That points to Eldorado

I can see the line
To find the shine
Of that place I need to go
I can see the money
I feel it in my tummy
I've found Eldorado.

**Hannah Rogers (10)**
**Oulton Broad Primary School, Oulton Broad**

## I Wonder Why

I wonder why a goat can bark
I wonder why outside is dark
I wonder why I have a mark
I wonder why I am called Clark
I wonder why my friend's called Pete
I wonder why I have a treat
I wonder if the world will stop
Before my mum pops to the shop!

**Harvey Farrow (8)**
**Oulton Broad Primary School, Oulton Broad**

## My Eldorado

*(Based on 'Eldorado' by Edgar Allan Poe)*

In the desert's heart
My journey will start,
I bleed and sweat,
Travelling so long,
Singing a song,
In my search for Eldorado.

But I grew old
Myself so bold,
I met a strange lonely horse,
Got on it of course
The sun such a great source,
To my quest for Eldorado.

But, as my strength
Failed me at length,
I saw a bright light,
I used my mind
To try and find
This land of Eldorado.

The weather was cold
I was getting old,
I starved and got weaker,
But around the next bend
I reached my journey end
I had found my Eldorado.

**Jack Townley (9)**
**Oulton Broad Primary School, Oulton Broad**

## I Wonder Why

I wonder why a lion goes roar
I wonder why some rooms have floors
I wonder why a dog can bark
I wonder why the space is dark
I wonder why camels like sand
I wonder why a plane can land
I wonder if the world will stop
Before my mum pops to the shop!

**Rio Howard (7)**
**Oulton Broad Primary School, Oulton Broad**

## Eldorado
*(Based on 'Eldorado' by Edgar Allan Poe)*

In the forest's heart
My journey I start,
Where ghosts are around
From this place I flee,
They're after me -
Where is my Eldorado?

As I ventured deep,
My heart began to weep
I climb upon my horse
He galloped round
As I frowned -
In search of Eldorado.

I'm growing old
Now not so bold
I meet a spirit
'Spirit,' said I
'Please don't lie,
Do you know of Eldorado?'

'Ride over the mountains
Off the stars,
Down the valley of despair,
Ride, boldly ride,'
The spirit replied -
'If you seek Eldorado!'

**Ella Cunningham (9)**
**Oulton Broad Primary School, Oulton Broad**

## I Wonder Why

I wonder why the moon can fly
I wonder why my friend said bye
I wonder why a mouse can squeak
I wonder why a dog can speak
I wonder why the Earth is great
I wonder why I like to wait
I wonder if the world will stop
Before my mum pops to the shop!

**Aidan Curtis (8)**
**Oulton Broad Primary School, Oulton Broad**

## My Eldorado
*(Based on 'Eldorado' by Edgar Allan Poe)*

In the meadow centre
I begin my adventure,
My horse chocolate brown,
Trotting along
Singing a song
In search of Eldorado.

But the time went fast
I feared I would not last,
Travelling over seas and mountains,
Towards a distance star,
But it was too far
Where is this land called Eldorado?

And as my strength weakened
The valley beckoned,
I met a willing ghost,
'Ghost,' said I,
'Where can it be
This land of Eldorado?'

Over the seas
Under the skies,
Down the valley of the mountain,
'Ride boldly ride,'
The ghost replied,
'If you seek for Eldorado.'

**Hannah Reid (9)**
**Oulton Broad Primary School, Oulton Broad**

## I Wonder Why

I wonder why a lion goes roar
I wonder why a crow can snore
I wonder why a rabbit can jump
I wonder why a head goes bump
I wonder why I like West Ham
I wonder why the wasps eat jam
I wonder if the world will stop
Before my mum pops to the shop!

**Ethan Nicolle (8)**
**Oulton Broad Primary School, Oulton Broad**

## Eldorado
*(Based on 'Eldorado' by Edgar Allan Poe)*

In the castle's heart
My journey will start
Dark and dull
The journey so long
Singing a song
In search of Eldorado.

I'm getting so old,
Still quite bold
But my body
Fell to ground
With no sign of land found
That looked like Eldorado.

My strength was going
When I heard something moaning
It was a pilgrim shadow
'Shadow,' said me
'Where could it be
This land of Eldorado?'

The shadow replied
'Ride, body, ride.'
Then I saw!
Some spot of ground
At last I had found
My magnificent Eldorado.

**Cameron Harbord (9)**
**Oulton Broad Primary School, Oulton Broad**

## I Wonder Why

I wonder why a cat can bike
I wonder why hamsters can hike
I wonder why a dog can bite
I wonder why a bird is light
I wonder why a bee says 'hi'
I wonder why we all must die
I wonder if the world will stop
Before my mum pops to the shop!

**Adam Seager (7)**
**Oulton Broad Primary School, Oulton Broad**

## My Eldorado
*(Based on 'Eldorado' by Edgar Allan Poe)*

In my nice little town
Me wearing the crown
My journey will start
On my milk coloured horse
I must keep on my course
In search of Eldorado.

My horse gets weaker up the mountain side
It tries not to slide
My armour is not helping
I'm getting older
And the mountain is getting colder
I must keep going in search of Eldorado.

I'm thinking of going back
Because the mountain might crack
But must keep going.
At the end of the day
I'm feeling okay
I meet a shadow in search of Eldorado.

He knows where to go
And now I know
It's not too long
I travel some more
And see the door
Which looks like Eldorado.

**Nathan Turrell (9)**
**Oulton Broad Primary School, Oulton Broad**

## I Wonder Why

I wonder why a moon is rock
I wonder why a moon is dock
I wonder why comets can shoot
I wonder why I have a boot
I wonder why Pluto is small
I wonder why I am so tall
I wonder if the world will stop
Before my mum pops to the shop!

**Sonny Anderson (8)**
**Oulton Broad Primary School, Oulton Broad**

## Eldorado
*(Based on 'Eldorado' by Edgar Allan Poe)*

In the forest's heart
My adventure will start,
Where cold dark spirits lurk
Away from home
I feel alone
In search of Eldorado.

The spirits lurked
As I worked
Screaming in my ears
No inch of ground
As I walked round
Looking for Eldorado.

As I got weaker
Then I went deeper
I never gave up
One spirit came
My horse to blame
Crying for Eldorado.

I saw some birds
I could not say any words
I must be close
Can I see
It must be
My beautiful Eldorado.

**Scarlet Banner (9)**
**Oulton Broad Primary School, Oulton Broad**

## I Wonder Why

I wonder why Pluto can spin
I wonder why there's such a din
I wonder why I like to go
I wonder why Santa goes 'ho'
I wonder why you turned off this
I wonder why this is a miss
I wonder if the world will stop
Before my mum pops to the shop!

**John McNamara (7)**
**Oulton Broad Primary School, Oulton Broad**

## Eldorado
*(Based on 'Eldorado' by Edgar Allan Poe)*

In the forest deep,
My journey I must keep
Cold and dark,
Towards a shady place,
I slow my pace,
In search of Eldorado.

But I grow so old,
Out in the cold
My journey goes on,
The days go slow,
As I quickly grow,
Where is this land of Eldorado?

When water is leaking,
The birds are squeaking
In darkness and light,
I look left and right,
But still no sight,
Of my Eldorado.

Over the tree tops,
Of the moon
Down the valley of shadows,
I'll show you now,
The shade replied,
If you seek for Eldorado.

**Kian Harvey (9)**
**Oulton Broad Primary School, Oulton Broad**

## I Wonder Why

I wonder why a mouse can see
I wonder why owls live in trees
I wonder why a cat can paw
I wonder why a lion can roar
I wonder why a crocodile snaps!
I wonder why sea lions clap
I wonder if the world will stop
Before my mum pops to the shop!

**Jack Kirk (8)**
**Oulton Broad Primary School, Oulton Broad**

## Eldorado

*(Based on 'Eldorado' by Edgar Allan Poe)*

In the valley's heart
My journey will start
Going through the gloom
Everything is quiet
I can't deny it
In search of Eldorado.

Hands from the ground
Are everywhere around
I am afraid,
Determined and
Seeking for this land
Called Eldorado.

A badger is here
Near the pier
He'll show me the way
For today
To find my Eldorado.

Happier than ever
As soft as a feather
Now I'm nearly there
It's as soft as a cloud
As I bowed
I have found my Eldorado.

**Amy Hoffman (9)**
**Oulton Broad Primary School, Oulton Broad**

## I Wonder Why

I wonder why a cat can fly
I wonder why a pig says hi
I wonder why rats come at night
I wonder why hamsters fly kites
I wonder why the light is bright
I wonder why rats at night fight
I wonder if the world will stop
Before my mum pops to the shop!

**Rebecca Braid (7)**
**Oulton Broad Primary School, Oulton Broad**

## My Eldorado

In a cave damp and dark
I will follow the mark,
Brick walls everywhere
Making a rhyme
It's all mine
As I search for Eldorado.

I'm getting older
Which makes me colder,
My heart is dropping down
With no sign of sight
It gave me a fright -
I think it's my Eldorado.

But then as I saw
It was just a boar
It felt like I was dead
I couldn't take a breath
I was in such a mess
He's a sign of Eldorado.

Through the cave
Of all these days
I could find Eldorado
'Now,' said he
'Why can't you see
It's my land of Eldorado.'

**Deren Karausta (10)**
Oulton Broad Primary School, Oulton Broad

## I Wonder Why

I wonder why a goat can bark
I wonder why a dog can snark
I wonder why a tiger chews
I wonder why a rat can snooze
I wonder why the Earth is dry
I wonder why the planets cry
I wonder if the world will stop
Before my mum pops to the shop!

**Thomas Riley (8)**
Oulton Broad Primary School, Oulton Broad

## Recipe For Making Adults Pleased

Offer to go shopping with a parent.
Ask to push your little brother.
Don't ask for anything in the shop.
Buy parent coffee.
Buy parent chocolate.
Go in clothes shop.
Pretend you're enjoying it more than football but you're not.
Put potatoes in bag before cream cakes.
Ask parent how much money she has.
Give her yours.
Say you don't need it back.
You're frustrated because brother's whinging.
Mum buys him a lolly, he stops.
Get on the bus.
Enjoy view.
Help pack everything away.
Cook tea.
Go to bed when told.
Give parents peace and quiet in morning.
Get parents their favourite breakfast.
Wash everything up.
Then they'll be happy.

**Harry Halstein (10)**
**Oulton Broad Primary School, Oulton Broad**

## I Wonder Why

I wonder why the flower grows
I wonder why the green grass blows
I wonder why the stars can shine
I wonder why a snail draws lines
I wonder why a horse eats hay
I wonder why some people play
I wonder if the world will stop
Before my mum pops to the shop!

**Erin Cook (7)**
**Oulton Broad Primary School, Oulton Broad**

## No Litter Please

I knew two girls,
Holly and Faith,
They were aged 13,
To the shop they raced.

They bought a sandwich each,
And chucked the rubbish on the beach,
The police came to take them away,
A fine they had to pay.

They went to the police station,
Their mum's got a ring,
'What have you done?'
The police had a gun.

The mum said sorry,
Then passed a lorry,
Then home they went
To their rooms they got sent.

**Tia Smith (10)**
**Oulton Broad Primary School, Oulton Broad**

## Recipe For Making Adults Pleased

Offer to go shopping with a parent.
Ask to carry the bags.
Ignore naughty brother.
Put bags in back of boot.
Push trolley back into shop.
Suggest something to eat and drink.
Go to café.
Help Mum up the stairs.
Offer to buy Mum coffee.
Feed baby brother.
Baby brother needs nappy changing.
Change it and put nappy in bin.
Come out of café.
Buy Mum a dress.
Go home and tidy house.
Mum's very pleased.

**Robert Flower (10)**
**Oulton Broad Primary School, Oulton Broad**

## Recipe For Making Adults Pleased

Offer to go shopping with a parent.
Don't ask for anything when you are in the shop.
Don't forget the shopping list that Mum said bring.
Offer to get a basket for Mum.
Don't wake the baby up!
Offer to go get half the food.
Offer to keep the baby asleep.
Offer to carry the bags.
Don't swing bag.
Try to keep food nice and neat.
Ask to go to the café.
Buy Mum a coffee.
Ask to go home.
Go home and do whatever you're told.
Get your pyjamas on and get ready for bed.
Go to bed immediately Mum says!

**Freya Easey (10)**
**Oulton Broad Primary School, Oulton Broad**

## Rain

Rain dribbled
Down the side of my window,
Blurred my view
Drowned each leaf and created loads of puddles -
Then he flushed down the gutter.

Rain drenched
My new coat,
Made me all wet,
Made me cold and made me shiver -
Then scurried on.

Rain flooded
The playground,
Made it wet play,
Soaked the field and made everywhere muddy -
Then filled the rivers to overflowing.

**Caitlin Farr (10)**
**Oulton Broad Primary School, Oulton Broad**

## Rain

Rain gushed
Down my window sill,
Blocking my way to see,
Drenched each tree and drowned each bug -
Then washed away.

Rain splashed
Down my spine
Lifting hair and hoods,
Ran down my top making me damp -
Then danced on.

Rain cascaded
Down the stream,
Lifting stones and mud,
On his face were sparkles,
Then he splashed away.

**Sophie Cooper (10)**
**Oulton Broad Primary School, Oulton Broad**

## Rain

Rain dripped
Down my windowpane
Blurred my view
Drowned each leaf and gulped each bug
Then shone in a pool.

Rain scattered
Around my garden
Feeding my flowers
Making them grow
And then sprinted along.

Rain travelled
Streamed down the playground,
Making it really slippery;
On her face were drips of water,
Making her really angry.

**Emily Hall (9)**
**Oulton Broad Primary School, Oulton Broad**

# Rain

Rain dripped
Down my windowpane
Stopped my view
Wiped out each leaf and hit every bug -
Then vanished into a pool.

Rain splashed
Down my face,
Making my eyes wet
Drinking the rain by accident -
Then I spat it out again.

Rain slapped
Down my car,
Making the vehicle shake
Made wipers run across the screen -
Then splashed onto the road.

**Travis Jacobs (9)**
**Oulton Broad Primary School, Oulton Broad**

# Rain

Rain hit
On my windowpane,
Blurred my view
Drowned each leaf and made insects
Then disappeared into a pool.

Rain raced
Down the car window
Hitting the vehicle loudly
Destroying the driver's view -
And then hurried off.

Rain danced
On the rainforest floor
Animals ran home
Plants drowned and animals got soaked -
Now his job was done.

**Josh Dixon (9)**
**Oulton Broad Primary School, Oulton Broad**

## Rain

Rain dripped,
On every leaf,
Touched each tree,
Dampened every bug -
Drenched even birds.

Rain crept,
Off every car,
Onto the pavement,
And into the drain -
One day I knew he would come out again.

Rain danced,
On my windowpane,
Into my room and under my bed,
Now his job was done.

**James Lawler (10)**
**Oulton Broad Primary School, Oulton Broad**

## Lost

The day at the beach was sunny
And the girl asked for some money.
The girl went to go and get some ice
Because that was rather nice.
When the girl went to go and get some ice
She got lost on the beach.
Oh no! She could not find her way back.
The police hunted night and day
But in the morning they started to play.
So when the girl got home
She looked around and sat down.
When her mum got home
She was excited to see the little girl
And she was relieved.

**Philippa Parr (9)**
**Oulton Broad Primary School, Oulton Broad**

## I Wonder Why

I wonder why a cat can fly
I wonder why a pig says bye
I wonder why a lion roars
I wonder why a goat has more
I wonder why a dog has fur
I wonder why a cat can purr
I wonder if the world will stop
Before my mum pops to the shop!

**Tegan-Elise Warren-Patterson (7)**
**Oulton Broad Primary School, Oulton Broad**

## I Wonder Why

I wonder why a rat can fly
I wonder why you say goodbye
I wonder why I like to ignore
I wonder why I am so bored
I wonder why snakes like to slither
I wonder why some frogs have sliver
I wonder if the world will stop
Before my mum pops to the shop!

**Thomas Betts (8)**
**Oulton Broad Primary School, Oulton Broad**

## I Wonder Why

I wonder why aliens blod
I wonder why UFOs tod
I wonder why a comet crashed
I wonder why a black hole smashed
I wonder why a rocket flies
I wonder why Neptune said hi
I wonder if the world will stop
Before my mum pops to the shop!

**Daniel Bowen (7)**
**Oulton Broad Primary School, Oulton Broad**

## I Wonder Why

I wonder why a dog can bark
I wonder why a light is dark
I wonder why I eat my snack
I wonder why I pack my sack
I wonder why I can fly fast
I wonder why I am not last
I wonder if the world will stop
Before my mum pops to the shop!

**Ethan Schroder (7)**
**Oulton Broad Primary School, Oulton Broad**

## Have You Heard Of This Stuff They Call Science?

Have you heard of this stuff they call science?
Why not buy some, unwrap it and try it?

It can shoot you straight up into the moon.
Clone a human? Not yet . . . but quite soon.

It can give your old granny a new plastic hip,
It can also float a humungous great ship.

It can restore the hair to your dad's balding head
And cryogenically freeze you the moment you're dead.

It can create a robot; full with a heart and a soul,
Prevent frogs from having to live on the dole!

It can trace a villainous thief with his own DNA
And contact aliens from worlds far, far away.

So the Earth with its global warming defiance,
To the everyday 'average-Joe' kitchen appliance.

But for the Earth and Mankind's most perfect alliance,
We're sure to need this great stuff they call science.

Just don't be afraid, crank your brain into gear,
If you use it correctly, there's nothing to fear.

So thanks to Einstein and his famous career
Be inspired by science and bring the future right here.

**Jacob Cameron (11)**
**Redcastle Furze Primary School, Thetford**

## On My Summer Holiday

Going on holiday, driving in our car,
All the family hope it is not far.

We want the sun to shine all day
So we can play in the golden sand . . .

Swimming underneath the sea would be
A lovely treat with all the crabs and fish
That I would like to meet.

Perhaps I would meet a mermaid
To play with all the time
And she might show me a treasure chest
That I would say was mine.

**Blossom May (8)**
**Redcastle Furze Primary School, Thetford**

## Mummy

Mummy, I love my dummy
Mummy, you are so yummy
Mummy, you are so scrummy like food in my tummy
I love my mummy
She's just so scrummy
I would love her to be in my tummy
But she's right here beside me
I love my mummy
Mummy, remember I love my dummy.

**Angel Lott (8)**
**Redcastle Furze Primary School, Thetford**

## My Secret Garden

Every day I visit my secret garden
All kinds of creatures come to greet me in a special way.
There are exotic trees and plants that sway in the breeze.
There is a waterfall that shimmers every time I dream.
Fairies flutter around me as they mutter to one another.
My secret garden is like no other.

**Sarah Watts (11)**
**St Felix School, Southwold**

## Incident In Barbados

I was sitting on the scorching beach
Waiting and waiting for the hire car.
We were off to travel all over Barbados.
Suddenly there was a man in the middle of the road
We stopped
The man said we couldn't go that way
He got into our car
I was worried
He told us his name was Shaun.
Dad started to lean forward
He saw he had a knife as a bottle opener
And a bottle of rum in his hand
Shaun told Dad to drive
He said he would show us some views.
We drove through some fields
My heart was racing inside me
We stopped at the cliff
Shaun smiled at me
I saw he had an awesome gold tooth
Dad took some pictures
I saw Shaun looking at the camera
I started to worry and fidget
I saw there was money involved
He asked Dad for some and left
I felt relieved to see him open the door
He ran
He did get our money
I will never forget that Barbados incident.

**Imogen Templer (10)**
**St Felix School, Southwold**

## School Work

I came in from break and sat at my desk
I looked at the work that had been put in front of me
English, maths, some science too
Some complicated,
Some easy!
I thought I should do . . .
The easy stuff first . . .
The hard last.
Yes that's a good idea,
I'll do that!
The easy, was easy,
The hard, was hard!
Brilliant that's it!
I've done it all!
Pleased and confident
I strode to my teacher's desk
He said, 'Well done!'
He gave me a tick and a star.
Challenge completed.
Art next,
I can't wait!

**Sam Ellis (11)**
**St Felix School, Southwold**

## My Little Sister Hollie The Singer

My little sister Hollie is a good singer.
When she's happy she sings.
When she is sad she sings.
She sometimes sings loudly.
She sometimes sings quietly.
She sings all day.
She sings at night.
She sings whatever mood she is in.
She sings when she is meant to be going to bed.
She sings in the bathroom.
She sings in the living room.
She sings everywhere.
My little sister Hollie is a good singer.

**Ellie Heil (11)**
**St Felix School, Southwold**

## Skiing . . . Skiing . . . Skiing . . .

I love skiing, how about you?
I can carve, parallel and freestyle too.
I can do 360 jumps, rails and that,
Even on the dry slope mat.
I like the smell of Frankfurters and chips,
It really does make me lick my lips
I like the cool breeze in my face,
Saint Anton is my favourite place.
Skiing down black 35,
It really does keep me alive.
Now I'm skiing down black 2,
It certainly is the hardest run to do.
Après ski will keep me awake,
Until the dawn is about to break.
I love skiing for the adrenaline rush,
Got to go now to catch the Lech bus.
Skiing . . . skiing . . . skiing . . .

**Grace Collen (10)**
**St Felix School, Southwold**

## Tidal Wave Roller Coaster

As I stand in the queue,
Adrenaline rushes through my body,
I climb into the raft,
Feeling all tingly from top to toe,
The ride begins.
Up, up and up we go,
I grab hold of Dad's hand,
Screams come from all around us.
Down we go,
Our faces pushed right back in the wind,
My stomach churning with excitement,
We come to a halt,
That was amazing,
I am drenched,
My clothes are soggy,
Even my pants!

**May Bandy (11)**
**St Felix School, Southwold**

## Arthur Is Forever

His name is Arthur.
He is 12 years old.
He is so cute and fluffy.
I walk him in the fields near my house.
He really dislikes cats and rabbits.
He hates the postman.
And fireworks too.
When he hears thunder
He always comes and hides under my bed.
He has often tried to run away
Luckily he comes back when I whistle him.
He loves children but he couldn't eat a whole one.
When he wants to lie down he walks round in a circle.
Then he's happy to sleep in his nice warm bed.
I think he is the right dog for me.
Arthur is forever!

**Olivia Ellis (10)**
St Felix School, Southwold

## I Love My Brother

I love my brother
And he's all mine.
Sometimes he breaks my heart
When he ignores me.
My brother sometimes is annoying
When he hides my things.
He loves to play with me
But when he loses he gets angry
He sometimes walks away
And I get really sad
But then he turns back up
And I'm really happy.
I love him very much
He loves me and I love him
I love my brother.

**Natasha Harlock (9)**
St Felix School, Southwold

## Global Warming

The young polar bear plays outside his snow den
He slides down the snow hills.
He's near the edge of the ice floe
He looks at pieces of ice drifting around in the water.
The platform he is standing on cracks,
He falls into the freezing blackness but he cannot swim.
He thrashes around in the sea but his muscles fade.
He starts sinking,
Falling down beneath the sheet of ice
Engulfed by the cold.
His mother rushes up
But cannot reach him.
He is a victim of the Arctic Sea
He is a victim of global warming . . .

**James Harris (10)**
St Felix School, Southwold

## My Triumph

It was silent
But before I knew it the beep had gone
And I exploded off the block.
Instantly I hit the water and started swimming.
My first few strokes were the most powerful
I put on an extra bit of speed and reached the wall.
I turned, pushed off and started swimming
By now I was getting tired.
Just then I couldn't see anybody
I realised I was either coming first or last
I put on a final sprint.
Suddenly the wall was looming up
I touched home, I looked around
I raised my fists in triumph.

**Ross Tolliday (10)**
St Felix School, Southwold

## Over The Top

When I signed up I thought it would be fun
But now I know that war is like this . . .
Biplanes soar over my head
People's screams haunt me
Bullets spray around
The noise of tanks scares me
Blood sprays everywhere
Endless gunfire
Rats run up my leg
Stale food
Shells bursting
I wish I had never joined
The commander leads the way
*Bang!*

**Edward Paulley (10)**
**St Felix School, Southwold**

## My Runaway Cat Tips

My cat Tips, he's black and furry,
He likes to make his tail all curvy.
Tips, he loves to catch lots of rats
Because he thinks he's king of all cats.
Tips he loves Felix cat food
But he's always in a bad mood.
Oh Tips I wish you hadn't run away,
Oh I do want to see you today!
Oh Tips I loved you so
Why, oh why did you have to go?
I don't know why you ran away
And made me sad this holiday.

**Ava Jackson (9)**
**St Felix School, Southwold**

## Roger The Rabbit

I had an old rabbit called Roger.
He was round, soft, cuddly and fluffy.
I woke up one morning and went to say hello
I noticed his cage had been attacked,
I knew he was gone
And he wouldn't be coming back.
Mum and Dad went searching,
I didn't want to go,
So I stayed inside.
I waited and waited,
But no good news came.
I felt heartbroken and empty inside.

**Lucy Clarke (9)**
St Felix School, Southwold

## I Call My Nanny Mrs Treat

I call my nanny Mrs Treat
Every day she comes to see me
With chocolate and mints for tea.
She cooks us food on a Sunday night
And when I'm asleep she tucks me up tight.
She also has a cheerful laugh
Which I know sounds a tiny bit daft.
Her wrinkled skin is very rough
But I think she's very tough.
She always smells like fresh flowers
But sometimes she sleeps for many hours.
I call my nanny Mrs Treat.

**Edith McKenna (10)**
St Felix School, Southwold

## A Great Day

I ride around on my yellow BMX bike
I'm off to see my friend.
I ride round the corner
There he is, waiting for me
We talk and then go to my house
We ride our bikes back the same way
It is turning into a great day.
We have some lunch
We play and climb up trees.
We kick the football right up high
Then it's time to say goodbye.

**Joseph Drake (10)**
**St Felix School, Southwold**

## Pops

He's a kind, friendly, loving grandad.
He's always there to help me,
He likes to take a nap any time of day,
He's someone nice to snuggle up with.
He makes me feel cosy and safe.
He looks after us when Mum and Dad are away.
If I get bored he plays football with me.
He likes to shave his hedges,
And likes to cut his grass,
He is my grandad
But I call him Pops.

**Harry Collins (10)**
**St Felix School, Southwold**

## Mean Sister

M ean to me most of the time.
E ntirely horrible
A n annoying person she definitely is.
N ice to me hardly ever!

S cars on my face from her
I njuries that will never go away.
S howing off to all her friends.
T o just annoy me.
E veryone knows she's a pain
R eally rude to everybody, my mean sister.

**Thomas Hood (10)**
St Felix School, Southwold

## PlayStations Are Fun

A PlayStation is fun
I play on a game called 'Gun'
It's great to play
All the day.
It's good to chat
To a friend called Pat
But your mum will say
Every day
Too much PlayStation
Is bad for you!

**Joseph Powell (9)**
St Felix School, Southwold

## Harry

Harry is my dog
He is very furry and tall
To me he is gorgeous and cute
He runs around the garden with his toy bunny
When we go on walks we throw sticks
He runs like a maniac.
He is funny when he leaps up and down
When I have food he pretends to be hungry
Sometimes he looks as if he will fly
Because he jumps so very high.

**Emily Summers (10)**
St Felix School, Southwold

## My Dog Tula

My dog Tula likes to go to sleep
She likes to lie on my feet.
She can be annoying when she licks me
Shaking her fur when she's been in the sea.
She chases me about
Barking very loudly when I shout.
She likes to be alone
Always having a big fat bone.
In my dad's truck she sits up tall
She's the best dog ever and is protective of us all!

**Archie Laughland (11)**
St Felix School, Southwold

## Swimming

S is for streamline with fly kick off the wall.
W is for water which is always welcoming.
I is for ice-cold water when the pool heater broke down.
M is for the mist on my goggles after training hard.
M is for the misery when I don't win.
I is for Individual Medley, it's a very exciting race.
N is for nerves that shiver down my spine.
G is for the Olympic Gold that I'm going to win one day.

**Madeleine Chambers (10)**
St Felix School, Southwold

## I Love My Guinea Pigs

My guinea pigs go binky when I play with them,
When I feed them they squeak loudly,
Their colour matches their names,
Fudge and Caramel,
When I hold them they shiver and tremble,
I tell them they're safe with me,
They get scared when my dad walks past them,
They think he's a monster,
Sometimes they run underneath the newspaper and hide,
My guinea pigs are special to me!

**Sophie Keal (11)**
**St Felix School, Southwold**

## Twist

We got her from a rescue centre when she was one.
She was fit and could jump over walls
But she's unable to do that anymore
Because she's lost her spring and is losing fur
But when my brother comes home she's like a puppy again
We're scared though because she's fourteen now
But we really hope she will live for longer.
I love Twist, our rescue dog.

**Thea Hall (10)**
**St Felix School, Southwold**

## [b] Computer Jargon [/b] <br/>

There's lots of computer jargon, <br/>
All meaning odd things. <br/>
HTML - Hypertext Mark-up Language, <br/>
Who came up with this idea? <br/>
This complex world of IT, <br/>
So confusing, stupid computer speak! <br/>
All this jargon in its own world, <br/>
Why do we have computer jargon? <br/>
Perhaps it's the Internet?

**Thomas Hill (10)**
**St Felix School, Southwold**

## Frightful Night

I awoke to hear the creak of my bed,
So I got up and bumped my head.
I heard the wind blow through the air
Then I got a sudden scare,
I shivered with fright away through the night
I was holding my duvet so very, very tight,
When the morning came I felt so bright
That I got through that frightful night.

**Archie Wallis (11)**
**St Felix School, Southwold**

## While I Sleep

The moon is very white
And so bright in the middle of the night.
Silver sparkles on the moon while I sleep
The darkness tries very hard to creep.
If everybody slept in the day
The space lovers would say hooray.
When the sun has risen in the sky
The moon has gone and said goodbye.

**Oliver Annis (9)**
**St Felix School, Southwold**

## The Ham-Jam-Jam-Ham Poem

There once was a girl named Sam
One day she ate some ham
She felt so sick
She gave herself a kick
And decided to eat some jam.

**Evelyn Howat (10)**
**Seething & Mundham Primary School, Seething**

## Blowing Winds

B eastly wind
L ow pressure wind
O n whispering days
W ild wind
I cy wind
N ervous, crying wind
G entle breeze

W aiting wind
I n the sky
N imbostratus clouds
D ancing wind
S himmering wind.

**Amelia McIntyre (7)**
**Seething & Mundham Primary School, Seething**

## Sunny

S un is great, sun is cool! Sun is fiery orange, sun is blinding but lastly, sun is a golden coin.
U sually sun is shiny and bright and it is relaxing gold, just like the shimmering eye of the glorious queen.
N ot just that, but it's also the burning orange piece of glass.
N o one knows how good the sun is, it's the glistening, blinding, boiling, burning sun.
Y ou always know that the sun's the best of all.

**Emily Storey (7)**
**Seething & Mundham Primary School, Seething**

## Ben

There once was a boy called Ben
Who saw a hen in his den
He locked it up
And gave it to the pup
So was arrested by policemen.

**Ryan Crowder-Barr (9)**
Seething & Mundham Primary School, Seething

## The Tree

There once was a boy called Will
Who had a friend called Squill
They swung in the trees
And got stung by bees
And Will ended up very ill!

**Eleanor Storey (9)**
Seething & Mundham Primary School, Seething

## Phil

There once was a boy called Phil
Who liked to jump on a mill
Oh dear, he fell off
Landed on a moth
That was the end of Phil!

**Louis Price (9)**
Seething & Mundham Primary School, Seething

## Spaghetti

There once was a lady called Betty
Who loved to suck on spaghetti
She met a bloke
Who made her choke
Then sped off in a Bugatti.

**Fenella Jenkins (10)**
Seething & Mundham Primary School, Seething

## Bob!

There was an old man called Bob
Who couldn't find a job
He went on a flight
To see the might
Of a big boss called Mob.

**Joshua Davies (10)**
**Seething & Mundham Primary School, Seething**

## Mr Hamster

There was a hamster who loved to eat
His friend, Rabbit, had 11 feet
He fell down a hole
And sat on a mole
And found out the mole's name was Pete.

**Annabel Wykes (10)**
**Seething & Mundham Primary School, Seething**

## Jill

There was a girl called Jill
Who felt very, very ill
So she went to the doctors
Who said, 'You've got the poxes!'
And so now she has pills.

**Lucy Mann (10)**
**Seething & Mundham Primary School, Seething**

## Fly

There was a boy called Fly
He loved to eat apple pie
He filled up his tummy
Then cried to his mummy
Because a wasp stung him in the eye.

**Siouxsie Littlewood (11)**
**Seething & Mundham Primary School, Seething**

## Snow

S wirling, curling snow, flying round the garden.
N ow it's sparkling round the trees.
O h no! It's stopped snowing.
W ell, it's nice to see the snow but not every day.

**Esme Walton (8)**
Seething & Mundham Primary School, Seething

## Wind

W hirling wind rustling the trees
I mposter wind making me cold
N agging wind pushing me over
D eadly wind making a hurricane.

**Sam Warren (9)**
Seething & Mundham Primary School, Seething

## Snow

S ugary, powdery snow
N othing sparkles like snow
O h no! The snow's gone
W hirling and swirling snow.

**Arwen Proctor (7)**
Seething & Mundham Primary School, Seething

## Sun

Bright sun in the sky,
Boiling hot, orangey-gold eye.
Bursting red flames glow.

**Rory Jackson (8)**
Seething & Mundham Primary School, Seething

## Rainforest Poem

Leopards leap
Monkeys swing
Tigers roar
Rain always pours
Okapis trotting through the woods
Looking for water and different foods
Blue, sparkly raindrops in the woods on this wonderful day
Wow! What a nice forest, let's go this way
Chip, chop, go the trees,
Snakes in the forest, oh gee!
Down in the jungle where nobody goes,
There's a big fat gorilla pickin' his nose.
There's a big snake
Teeny-tiny flowers, monkeys are the cowards,
Parrots fly, sugar gliders glide,
Bye-bye rainforest, Egypt's king is Horus,
Plants are growing, people are sowing,
Run from the gorillas, run from the snakes,
And don't do a big mistake.
So run, run, go home,
Lock your doors and go under your beds.

**Julia Vickova (8)**
**Weeting Primary School, Weeting**

## The Rainforest

Leopards leap,
Monkeys swing,
Tigers pounce,
Plants growing,
Sun shining.

Rain vibrating on the soft, muddy ground
Blossoms opening, their sense of smell
Hummingbirds collecting nectar
Red and blue
A fantastic hue
People hunting wild animals
What would you do?

**Charlie Long (7)**
**Weeting Primary School, Weeting**

## The Best Friend Ever

T he best friend,
H appy and heartful,
E nergetic and bubbly.

B ecause she's mine,
E xpressing her emotions,
S he never wants to cry,
T he best friend is mine.

F ight, we've never had one.
R ed, she does not like.
I n time we will be one,
E verything we've done.
N ever, ever ends together,
D one it now, don't go back.

E ven when
V iolet turns red,
E ven the
R oses are ours.

**Cara Solomon (11)**
**Weeting Primary School, Weeting**

## The Rainforest

Monkeys leap,
Crocodiles snap,
Tigers sprint,
Green plants,
Red flowers,
Blue rivers,
Sparkle round,
Blue rain,
Pitter-patter,
Coming down,
Need shelter?
Mean men,
Cutting trees,
Deforestation equals
*Bad!*

**Ellie-May McCreedy (7)**
**Weeting Primary School, Weeting**

## The Tall, Scary Pirate

T all
A wful
L egendary
L iar

S cary
C old
A ngry
R ude
Y oung

P roud
I ncredible
R ebel-like
A nnoying
T errifying
E xcellent

The tall, scary pirate.

**Gaby Holder (10)**
**Weeting Primary School, Weeting**

## My Best Friends

My friends are funny,
Pretty, kind and caring,
They are as cool
As ice, but on the

Inside they are as
Warm-hearted as the
Sun. I feel so
Lucky, lucky like a

4-leaf clover.
My friends are the best.
I will take care
Of my friends

And I will have
Them by my side
Forever!

**Samantha Smith (10)**
**Weeting Primary School, Weeting**

## Hasto, The Great Statue

The tall statue is:
Cold and lonely,
Old and hard,
Tall and naked,
Tall and man-like,
Stony and blue.
Hasto is thinking:
*It's not very nice without clothes!*
*I need clothes!*
Hasto is also thinking:
*I'm tall, white, weird and high.*
Hasto wants to dive in the sea.
*I need some clothes on,*
*Some stripy and stiff clothes.*

**Jordan Rhodes (9)**
**Weeting Primary School, Weeting**

## Hasto Statue

H asto needs clothes
A lot of them,
S tripy and stiff,
T he statue is thinking of diving into the sea,
O ld but hard the statue is.

S ad,
T owering,
A nd not very nice,
T hinking of diving in, he is,
U nlikely to get forgotten,
E ven though he is old.

**Chris Pope (11)**
**Weeting Primary School, Weeting**

## My Classroom In Weeting

The classroom that stands in the
Middle of Weeting,
Is not to be scared of,
There is lots of seating.
There are people kind and hard to find,
But they will always be there for you.
There are people funny,
As funny as a clown and Weeting
Is next to Brandon town.
The classroom that stands in the
Middle of Weeting.

**Emily Moore (11)**
**Weeting Primary School, Weeting**

## As Big As The World

I'm a big and great statue,
I'm incredible and tall,
It makes me feel tall and proud,
People call me fantastic and the great white life,
People say, 'This statue is great!'

Some people pray for me and love me,
Other people think I'm a waste of space.
I sometimes feel sad and upset,
I hope most people like me and pray.
A man said to me, 'You're my hero.'

**Danny Juniper (11)**
**Weeting Primary School, Weeting**

## Hasto The Great Statue

The statue is:
Tall, old, naked, weird, high,
White, stripy, stiff, hard, happy,
Stony, bluey-green, man-like.
The statue is thinking of diving in the sea,
'I need some clothes on!'

**Jessica Baker (10)**
**Weeting Primary School, Weeting**

## The Sphinx

It makes me feel excited,
Small, scared, amazed, ancient,
Like I'm in the Egyptian times.
It's like it's protective of the little statues
Between its feet.

The little statue is probably thinking
*When can I sit down?*
And the big statue is thinking
*What a great view I have
For I am the sphinx.*

**Alicia Drewry (10)**
**Weeting Primary School, Weeting**

## The White Lady

How glamorous I look.
I'm the best of them all.
I make people feel small.
Humans respect me.

I'm huge, heroic and phenomenal.
I may be old but I'm very pretty.
People think I'll fall over, I'm so big.

**Max McCreedy (11)**
**Weeting Primary School, Weeting**

## My Friend

My friend is called Mia,
I've known her since I was four.
She's OK, a bit of a pain,
But she's my friend.
She's as loud as an elephant,
As jumpy as a jumping bean.

I feel very happy about my friend, Mia,
As happy as a hippo, my friend.
I need my friend because without her
I'd be very lonely.

**Destiny Back (10)**
**Weeting Primary School, Weeting**

## Bongos, Bongos

Bongos, bongos, have you ever wanted to hear the sound?
Bongos, bongos, have you ever wanted to see your grandma dance so much that she hits the ground?

Bongos, bongos, people talk about them all day,
Bongos, bongos, people play them in such a way.

Bongos, bongos, you can play them anywhere,
Bongos, bongos, you won't give anyone a scare.

Bongos, bongos, hit them with all your might,
Bongos, bongos, please don't start a fight.

**Libby Brockett (10)**
**Weeting Primary School, Weeting**

## The No Clothes Man

Naked man
I'm so cold
It makes me want to explore the world
Makes me feel uncomfortable
Wish people would stop staring at me
Big, strange to look at
Put some clothes on, please
Scary and distressing
Worried, scared and probably cold
Something weird and solid.

**Joseph Dilley (10)**
**Weeting Primary School, Weeting**

## The Great Dragon Of China

I'm Hastie, the great dragon of China,
I'm fantastic, big, astonishing, gold but very expensive,
I'm really bored because all I do is just sit here all day,
I'm really frightened and scared,
But I'm fearful, spiky, golden, like a golden retriever,
I'm a fire dragon,
Spiky, scary, big, gold and really lonely,
Once again, I'm Hastie, the great dragon of China.

**Ryan Aves (10)**
**Weeting Primary School, Weeting**

### The White Lady

How magnificent I look.
I'm matchless.
I make people feel calm
Because I'm so massive.
People respect me.
I'm so massive, scary, strong and wide.
I'm old,
I'm over 1,000 years old.
People think I will fall over
Because I'm so massive.

**Lewis Wells (9)**
**Weeting Primary School, Weeting**

## The Sphinx

It makes me feel so excited,
Scared, amazed, magnificent,
Ancient like I'm in Egyptian times.
It's protecting the small statue between his big feet.
It's so big it makes me feel like an ant.
It makes me feel scared,
Everyone staring at me for thousands of years.
But what a great view I have!

**Alicia Frost (11)**
**Weeting Primary School, Weeting**

### My Best Friend

Her name is Daisy,
She is so lazy,
She is crazy.

When we fight,
She has heroic might,
And everything works out alright.

When we say sorry,
We always watch Corrie
And then we never worry.

**Naomi Hadnum (11)**
**Weeting Primary School, Weeting**

## No Clothes Statue

I'm cold.
It makes me want to explore the world.
He makes me small.
It makes me feel uncomfortable.

I wish people wouldn't stare at me.
Naked man.
Big, strong and solid,
Stripped and worried.
Where are my clothes?

**Charlie Stone (11)**
**Weeting Primary School, Weeting**

## Washing Tomarni

I am fierce, I look like a lion,
But I'm actually a dragon.
I'm spiky, huge and lethal.
I'm powerful and angry.

People think I'm golden and divine,
People jump out of their socks when they see me.
People get cold when they see me.
They flee as quickly as they can.

I am Washing Tomarni.

**Daniel Buonocore (11)**
**Weeting Primary School, Weeting**

## The Beast Of China

I'm Hasto, the beast of China.
Fabulous, grand, astonishing, gold.
I'm bored because all I do is sit there.
I frighten people,
Scare them and worry them.
I'm fierce, spiky, golden,
Like a golden retriever.
They call me fire dragon
For I am Hasto.

**Charles Smith (11)**
**Weeting Primary School, Weeting**

## I Feel As Big As The World

I'm big, phenomenal, incredible and massive
I feel proud because I can stand tall and please everyone.
Everyone calls me White Life,
People talk on phones saying,
'I've been waiting here for ages . . .
Where are you?'
And I say, 'You don't know what's waiting for ages.'
I sometimes feel curious
And it's unusual for me to feel curious.

**Catalina Lis (10)**
**Weeting Primary School, Weeting**

## Rainforest Poem

Leopards leap and roar
The rain pours down
Plants grow in the rainforest
Tigers roar really loudly *Roar!*
Monkeys go *ho-ho, ha-ha,*
Parrots go *ork, ork, ork*
Gorillas go *hoo, hoo, hoo*
Pitter-patter goes the rain in the
*Rainforest!*

**Eleanor Vaughan (7)**
**Weeting Primary School, Weeting**

## Last Year!

Last year I saw Luke do a big puke.
Last year I saw Joe eating his own toe.
Last year I saw Jordan having a fight with Gordon.
Last year I saw Rew racing a kangaroo.
Last year I saw Jake trip and fall into a lake.
Last year I saw James losing on all his games.
Last year I saw Ellie eating a wellie.
Last year I saw Sinead put a grenade in lemonade.
Last year I saw Brianna eating Rhianna.
That all happened last year.

**Jordan Reader (10)**
**West Earlham Junior School, Norwich**

## True Love

When I see your eyes
I stop and stare
It's like the moonlight
Within my care
When you put your hair down
Under the glistening stars
It shines far away
Even from Mars
Your smooth hand touched me
Under the tree
We gazed at each other
While sitting by the sea
I love the girl
With all my heart
Until we
Flew right apart
I tried to hold on
With my strong hand
Until I lost grip
And flew into the sand
On that horrible night
I lost the girl of my dream
My heart is now broken
My tears formed a stream.

**James Goldie (10)**
**West Earlham Junior School, Norwich**

## The Vikings Came

The Vikings came
Defiantly, courageously,
Angrily, wildly,
Loudly, madly,
Crashing, bashing,
Smashing, fighting,
Rowing, rocking,
Across the
Wild, mad sea
To England.

**Rafa Nazim (7)**
**West Earlham Junior School, Norwich**

## Slave Traders

I met him while I was farming
He seemed the caring type
But that was an epic mistake
That cost my freedom and my life.

He said his name was Kovu
He invited me to lunch
He said, 'What's the worst that could happen?'
And gave me a friendly punch.

After all the excitement
We went to his place
He asked me to come and see his boat
Down by the shimmering, sparkling lake.

At first I thought it was kindness
But soon I knew the truth!
My great primate ancestors told me
I felt it in my African roots.

I turned around to run
Alas, I was too late
Kovu sold me to an American
I thought he was my mate!

He laughed at me with joy
I thought life was no longer fair!
He whipped me on and off the decks
And pulled off all my hair.

I thought, *why did I trust him?*
*How could I be so dumb?*
I missed my brothers and sisters
But especially missed my mum!

I felt as dreadful shock
A shiver down my spine
Will I end up dropping down dead
Or will I stay alive?

I want to commit suicide
I want to starve to death
Life is not worth living
And I think I'm going deaf!

I feel all alone
In this cold and lonely place
I once saw a future
Now it's just a haze.

One day I'll escape
Finally, I'll have rights!
Finally, I'll be able to sleep once more
And see my tribal lights.

**Rwanda Wilkerson (10)**
**West Earlham Junior School, Norwich**

## My Best Friend

I went to the countryside one day
That day changed my life
I felt the wind pushing onto my face
I thought it was telling me something
I stepped onto the green grass and put my arms out wide
I closed my eyes and imagined
I imagined my best friend was standing by my side
I opened my eyes and a little girl was near a tree
I went to say hi
But when I got there it was just a memory floating in the air
At that minute she was my best friend
We still meet at that countryside
With the wind pushing onto my face
And that bright green grass with the girl by the tree
I go there every day
Every day of my life
I wonder if she is still there
Under the tree of imagination
She still stands
But I wish she was there.

**Whitney Dunthorne (10)**
**West Earlham Junior School, Norwich**

## When The Orange Ate The Pig

There was a young man who swallowed a pig,
It wasn't that big, so he swallowed a pig.
There was a young man who swallowed an orange,
Who ate a pig that wasn't so big.
There was a young man who swallowed a tree,
Who swallowed the orange, who ate the pig that wasn't that big.
There was a young man who swallowed a car,
Who ate a tree, who swallowed the orange,
Who ate the pig that wasn't that big.
There was a young man who swallowed a double-decker bus,
Who ate a car, who ate a tree,
Who swallowed the orange,
Who ate the pig that wasn't so big.
There was a young man who ate the Eiffel Tower,
Who swallowed a double-decker bus,
Who ate a car, who ate a tree,
Who swallowed the orange,
Who ate the pig that wasn't so big.
There was a young man who eventually died,
For eating six things he shouldn't have tried!

**Luke Chamberlain (11)**
**West Earlham Junior School, Norwich**

## Basketball

B ouncing the ball across the slippery, shiny floor
A skilful dribble to our players
S coring baskets for our team
K indly passing to our team-mates
E nough is enough, we are losing 4-2
T ime is running out!
B ouncing, bouncing up the court and dribble
A nd winning the fabulous games with a lay up
L aughing as the crowd goes wild, screaming and shouting
L eaping up to say we are the champions!

But it's not all about winning
It's about participating
Bouncing, bouncing, bouncing . . .

**Charmaine Storey (11)**
**West Earlham Junior School, Norwich**

## Ember

The fire keeps burning
Fifth morning today
But the eyes are still glimmering
It still keeps burning
Flame by flame
Every day the fire still crackling
The flames blaze
Go on and on
Finally it stops
My heart still beating
It starts to die out
A swarm of embers swirl up in the air
What's left of the fire crackles
Alone in the dark, all that's left are sparks of embers
While this fire's dead, another's sparking into light
And millions more, all burning light together.

**Joseph Kuta (10)**
**West Earlham Junior School, Norwich**

## I Love Cricket

I love to play cricket,
I always hit the wicket.
I bowl as fast as the speed of light,
When I hit the ball it goes for a long flight.

I love to hit spin,
So we're sure to win.
I'm a superb all-rounder
And a cricket ball pounder.

I'm a cricket ball shooter
And a wicket stealing looter
For Crystal Palace my cus is Neil Danns
But I have lots of cricket plans.

**Wisdom Danns (10)**
**West Earlham Junior School, Norwich**

## Poem

Little Jack Horner
Sat in the corner
Picking his little pink nose,
He said, 'It's amazing!
It looks like a raisin
And tasted as good I suppose.'

It's green and black,
It's round and fat,
There's lots up that little pink nose.
He picks it, he licks it,
Then he flicks it.
He says, 'Oh, I miss that green sticky thing now.'

**Sinead Hoban (11)**
**West Earlham Junior School, Norwich**

## The Vikings Came

The Vikings
Came aggressively,
Madly, sailing,
Rocking, rolling,
Smashing, crashing,
Plundering, attacking,
Banging, fighting,
Across the deep sea
To England.

**Jessica Day (8)**
**West Earlham Junior School, Norwich**

## The Viking

The Viking
Came angrily, cautiously,
Sailing, rowing,
Rocking, tossing,
Smashing, crashing,
Plundering, attacking,
Thundering, yelling,
Bashing across
The dark, wavy sea.

**Sarah Muhammad (7)**
**West Earlham Junior School, Norwich**

## The Rainforest

The rainforest is sparkly
As creatures glow.
The rain falling down
On the animals below.

The noise is very loud
As the creatures all sing,
The birds in the trees,
The snakes down below.

The monkeys are very cheeky,
Swinging in the trees,
Doing their funky moves,
So all their friends can see.

The spiders running around,
On the forest ground,
Trying to catch their prey
In any way.

The night is here,
The noise goes away.
The forest is sleeping,
Ready for a new day.

**Ryan Surridge (8)**
**West Row Community Primary School, West Row**

## The Hedgehog's Day

There once was a hedgehog who had prickles
And his name was Mr Tickles
He snuffles while he shuffles
He speaks while he sleeps
He was in the shade and ice cream was made
He played and prayed
He played in the shade while drinking lemonade
He lay in the sun while eating a bun
He ran on his paw with a straw
He fell on his face and landed in this massive place
He spent his money on his favourite food - honey
He hurt his ear and we saw a tear
He saw a truck driven by a duck
And it was stuck in some muck
He thought he was dreaming
But he was actually cleaning
He saw a frog in the fog on a log
He went out and with his snout smelt a sprout
He forgot to get a net for his friend
His friend was upset
He saw a bowl with a pole and a mole in a hole
He saw a hen with a man called Ken
With his pen and his son, Ben
He saw the queen with her green telly screen
While she screamed
He loves tricks and he likes licks
And he was the happiest hedgehog in the land.

**Aimee Flack (8)**
**West Row Community Primary School, West Row**

## Football

Football's great, it keeps me fit,
I have a bright red England kit.
Football's great, it gives me thrills,
It teaches me many skills.
I use control when I dribble,
I can chip the ball up the middle.
We start the game from the centre spot,
I run up the pitch to take the shot.
I fly past defence and shoot at goal!
I play the game with my heart and soul.
The ball curved past the bright white post,
The goalie thought he'd seen a ghost!
It smashed its way through the net,
My coach was able to header it.
Football's great, I love the game,
Even though it drives Dad insane.

**Jack Merrill (8)**
**West Row Community Primary School, West Row**

## The Hungry Spaceman

Spaceman is on the moon,
Eating cake with a spoon.
Spaceman saw a star go past,
It went by very fast.
Then spaceman found his way to Mars
And wanted to eat chocolate bars!
But he couldn't get it through his mask,
It really was a tricky task!
Then he left Mars in a hurry
And flew home to eat some curry.

**Brendan Price (7)**
**West Row Community Primary School, West Row**

## Friendship

Everyone needs a friend or two
Maybe help them tie their shoe.
It doesn't matter if they're big or small,
Or even really, really tall.
If they're feeling really sad and lonely,
You're not the only one.
Make your friendship always last,
Don't get angry and run really fast.
Friendship is the best thing to have,
Yes it is, yes, yes, yes!

**Lyndon Dozier (7)**
**West Row Community Primary School, West Row**

## A Visit To The Circus

Acrobats way up high,
Acrobats high in the sky.
The crowd hold their breath,
As they know a fall could mean death.
The acrobat is safely lowered down,
The applause could be heard throughout town.

Clowns as funny as comedians,
Throwing water on each other,
Driving silly cars around the ring,
I wish they would throw water on my brother!

Amazing magicians, breathtaking to watch,
Turning a book into honey
And then a bunny!
How they do it I do not know.
Everyone claps and shouts, 'Woah!'

When it's over and it's time to go,
Everyone shouts, *'No, no, no!'*
When I went to sleep,
Dreaming very deep,
I was thinking about the clown with the big red nose.
But why? Only God in Heaven knows.

**Laila Chaudhry (9)**
**West Winch Primary School, King's Lynn**

## The Beauty Of The Circus

I remember my first visit to the circus,
Oh yes, I remember it so well,
Shining in a muddy field lies the big top tent,
A beauty, like a star in the sky.

So colourful, like a kid's first birthday,
It is a spinning top on a black table.
As I approached the door, millions of kids were there,
Screaming, shouting, at the smell of sweets.

As you enter you get a crazy feeling,
Well, you are teased by toy sellers,
Toy sellers with their toys so bright,
And hot dog stalls. Oh, they smell so nice!

Inside then. There's a giant shout,
And that's when the ringmaster's about.
He says, 'Let the show begin.'
The audience give him a big grin.

A clown rides around on a unicycle,
Spraying you with water like an elephant.
Up above the lights shine on, look
Tightrope walkers! About fifteen feet high.

Suddenly, something happens, swinging from a rope,
Around the room, like a flying dove, she soars.
A trapeze artist is she, why, the thrill is rising,
In the circus every minute is so exciting.

The end is near, the children sob,
But then everyone, even the ringmaster, got together.
It was a parade, with the music louder than ever,
Oh, what a lovely night. It was the best!

**Lily Davidson (8)**
**West Winch Primary School, King's Lynn**

# When I Went To The Circus

When I went to the circus,
I thought of the crowd
Roaring with laughter,
Would make me proud.

I sat on the bench,
Waiting for it to begin.
I saw the popcorn,
Smelling like parkin.

Now it's beginning,
I saw the ringmaster.
When he announced acrobats and tightropes,
I thought it would be a disaster!

But it was not,
They were trained.
Jumping and flipping,
I was amazed!

Now for the clowns,
They aren't the same.
Throwing pies made me think,
What a game!

Now for the trapeze artist,
Flying away.
That is not something,
You would see every day.

Last of all,
The magic show.
In a hat,
A vanishing doe!

Now it's home time,
If you would like,
But if they're so awesome,
I'll stay here tonight

Because of the workshop,
It is great,
Juggling, spinning plates,
And patterns to create.

Now it's really the end,
I said goodbye,
I travelled back home, I felt a tear,
I missed the circus but it will be here next year.

**Dayna Edwards (8)**
**West Winch Primary School, King's Lynn**

## Circus

Look at the clown, look at the clown,
With the great big frown,
No more jokes, no more jokes for the huge, giant crowd.

We sit there, we sit there,
With our mouths wide open,
No more words, no more words
Are even spoken.

Look at the magicians, look at the magicians
Turning the rabbits into -
However do they do that?
That's not so plain!

Look at the contortionists, look at the contortionists
Bending their hands,
Backwards and forwards,
Like elastic bands!

Look at the tightrope walker, look at the tightrope walker
Balancing on that rope,
However does he do that?
I could not cope!

Look at the crowd, look at the crowd
Holding their breath,
You do know -
This could mean death!

**Millie Rattenbury (8)**
**West Winch Primary School, King's Lynn**

## The Entire Circus

Fire-eaters look awesome and cool,
Makes the tightrope walker look a fool.

Stunts are risky and full of fear,
When they scream it hurts my ear.

At the big top they sell hot dogs,
They make magic in puffs of fog.

The audience are cheering,
The magician is disappearing.

All the magic is coming inside me,
With excitement, laughter and glee.

The acrobats are jumping like a rubber band,
Then a magician held out his hand.

The little red bike, with a loud horn,
Made me feel tired and made me yawn.

It's all over now, when I start to cry,
I'm not faking or telling a lie.

**Joe Pearce (8)**
**West Winch Primary School, King's Lynn**

## Circus

The circus tent opened and the people sat,
The funny clown was dressed like a rabbit.

Out came the fire-eater, he ate the fire like soup,
The trapeze artists bending their bodies like snakes.

Here the ringmaster stands,
In the centre of the tent the ringmaster shouts.
The tightrope walker tries not to look down,
A magician makes an elephant into a mouse.

The audience shouts, 'Bravo!' for each act.
The lion's roar scared everyone.
Now the circus tent stands alone,
Like a beautiful fairy castle.

**Eknath Manoj (9)**
**West Winch Primary School, King's Lynn**

## Feelings For The Circus

We pay the money,
For them to act funny.
Our mouths are wide open,
While no words are spoken.
In here it is bright,
But outside it is night.

The wheels fell off the car,
So it didn't travel very far.
We are down low,
But up high is the show.
All the crowd,
Are shouting loud.

When the crowd cheer,
It's their release from fear.
Everyone shouts, 'Look, look!
What's the magician took?'
A dove from the air,
Now it will disappear!

**Susannah Murray (8)**
**West Winch Primary School, King's Lynn**

## Clowns

Clowns are tall,
Clowns are small,
Clowns hit the wall,
When they bounce a ball.

Clowns like yellow,
Clowns like red,
Clowns like paint,
Oh! What a mess!

Clowns are funny,
Clowns are sunny.
Clowns make me laugh,
Because they are daft!

**Natasha Denney (9)**
**West Winch Primary School, King's Lynn**

## Dazzling Circus

The magician, with his assistant by his side,
The horses, with their guide.
The clowns throwing a bit
Of candyfloss from a stick.

The audience cheering,
The ringmaster hearing,
And taking a bow,
Say, 'Our show's over now!'

But come back next year,
'Cause there'll be more danger and fear!
Then the audience cheered some more,
Even though the dazzling circus was done for.

So the audience left in their groups,
For the stunning circus' troops,
Were grabbing their mop
And cleaning the big top.

**Jasmine Reeve (8)**
**West Winch Primary School, King's Lynn**

## The Circus Of Fun

When I went to the circus of fun
I couldn't believe my eyes
There were clowns smudging pies in their faces
The amazing tightrope walker
I hoped they wouldn't fall today!
Magicians making rabbits come out of a hat
I wonder how they do that!
The ringmaster commanding the crowd
So the crowd made a really big sound
Jugglers juggling with 1, 2, then 3
The fire-eaters swallowing fire
Spitting it out higher and higher!
'Hooray! Hooray!' screamed the crowd
At last the trapeze arrived
When they did some unbelievable stunts
The audience cheered and shouted!
I just hope I go again!

**Zack Crouch (9)**
**West Winch Primary School, King's Lynn**

## The Circus Is Coming To Town

The circus is coming to town
I hope the divers don't drown,
The clowns I can't wait to see,
They always seem to spot me.

The audience will be roaring,
While they are performing,
The trapeze artists are in the air,
The clowns are pulling their hair.

The ringmaster will be leading,
With the tightrope walkers heeding,
The clowns are all messing about,
The audience will shout.

The lions roar loudly,
The ringmaster calls, 'Howdy!'
The ponies run free
And Silly Billy, the clown, spots me!

**Jessica Key (10)**
**West Winch Primary School, King's Lynn**

## The Circus

If you go to the circus you will see:
Lots of things that make you shout with glee!
You'll see magicians doing scary magic,
If someone fell from the tightrope it would be quite tragic!

Contortionists as bendy as an elastic band,
Sometimes there are clowns playing in the sand.
You'll see lots of different clowns doing different tricks,
The audience applauds at the stunning high kicks.

The kids laugh at the clowns, who are quite funny,
As a sweet smell goes across the crowd that smells like honey.
The kids at the front eat the candyfloss,
While the clowns shout at the boss.

**Corey Edmunds (9)**
**West Winch Primary School, King's Lynn**

## The Circus

The circus clown is having a joke,
He's a real funny bloke,
The stuntmen doing heart-stopping tricks,
One of them did the splits.

The brave fire-eaters playing with fire,
While the acrobats are swinging higher and higher,
The loud music playing away,
While a magician turns a dove into clay.

The audience giving huge applause,
As the acts leave through the doors,
Some of the children are going home,
As they eat their ice cream cones.

The circus is leaving,
I have memories for dreaming,
Can't wait till next year,
Because, of course, I'll be there.

**Owen Case (9)**
**West Winch Primary School, King's Lynn**

## When I Went To The Circus

When I went to the circus and saw that light,
I always knew it'd be a sight.
The acrobats were in the air,
But the clowns were down in despair.

The bareback rider was on his horse,
He knew what he was doing all day of course.
The ringmaster shouts all the way,
While the crowd calls.

The fire-eaters got the tent smoking,
But the clowns were still joking.
When the ringmaster said, 'Goodbye everyone.'
I just said, 'That was fun.'

**Tom English (9)**
**West Winch Primary School, King's Lynn**

## My Perfect Circus

At my perfect circus there would be:
Acrobats like jumping fleas,
Cartwheels so very speedy,
Handstands for minutes,
And the audience clapping to their limits.

At my perfect circus there would be:
Children laughing, exclaiming,
'They're so clumsy,
When they fall on the ground!
They throw water all around.'

It's the end of the show,
Oh no! Oh no! How awful,
We will come back again
And you will perform to the music's refrain.

For I feel I want to cry,
That's my perfect circus, goodbye.

**Sarah Wren (8)**
**West Winch Primary School, King's Lynn**

## When I See The Big Top

When I go to see the big top,
It seems like all of the acts never stop,
I've been to the circus once before,
I loved it so much that I begged to see more.

When I go to see the big top,
It seems like the acrobats never flop.
I love it when all the clowns are joking,
I laugh so much, it feels like I'm choking.

When I go to see the big top,
The clowns jump in the water and plop,
But soon when it's time to go,
You can hear the crowd shouting, 'Oh!'

**Elizabeth Curcillo (9)**
**West Winch Primary School, King's Lynn**

## The Circus

Amazing acrobats always in the air,
Terrific trapeze artists turning topsy-turvy,
Beautiful prancing ponies galloping around,
Fantastic, funny clowns throwing pies in the air.

Stunning costumes shining in the light,
The excited crowd cheering all around,
The ringmaster looking up in the air,
The bare-back rider jumping everywhere.

Two jugglers juggling saws in the air,
Brilliant tigers jumping through hoops,
Colourful lights shining so bright,
Five amazing fire-eaters, hot, hot, hot!

**Rosie Huang (8)**
**West Winch Primary School, King's Lynn**

## The Circus Countdown

10 trapeze artists flying through the air.
9 acrobats flipping over the stair.
8 fire-breathers breathing like bears.
7 tightrope walkers balancing in the air.
6 magicians turning a card into a hare.
5 clowns are acting as the children stare.
4 dancers dancing like a bear.
3 ringmasters arguing over a pear.
2 sea lions bouncing a ball on their head.
1 clown going to bed.

**Thomas Mason (9)**
**West Winch Primary School, King's Lynn**

## Circus

The horses bowing and trotting,
The magician daring,
The acrobats alarming,
The crowd gasping,
The clowns joking,
The ringmaster demanding,
The fire-eaters burning,
The animals roaring,
The tent is massive,
And tightrope walkers as careful as can be.

**Connor Wells (8)**
**West Winch Primary School, King's Lynn**

## The Circus

Fiery, fire-eaters
Glowing in the dark.
Colourful clowns,
As happy as a lark.
Agile acrobats,
With curious acts.
Genius jugglers,
Juggling hats.

All inside the big top.

**Dhaanish Mishal (8)**
**West Winch Primary School, King's Lynn**

## The Circus

The ponies' eyes dazzle as they jump through the ring of fire.
They do backflips, they do stunts on bikes.
The trapeze artists are spectacular as they fly thro' the air
And I can smell the popcorn.
The audience applaud.
Jaws drop in excitement
As we watch the fire-eaters eating fire.
Spectacular magic and colourful costumes.
Funny clowns playing pie in the face!

**Alex Grimes (8)**
**West Winch Primary School, King's Lynn**

## The Circus

A is for acrobats flipping through the air.
B is for balloons popping in your hair.
C is for chocolate eating in your chair.
D is for dancers like never seen before.
E is for excitement as tigers *roar!*
F is for fire as hot as spice.
G is for gorillas juggling balls.
H is for home time.

And that is how the circus ends!

**Rudi Stevens (9)**
**West Winch Primary School, King's Lynn**

## Circus Acts

Clowns throwing pies,
What a surprise!
Tightropers walking,
Lions stalking
And the ringmaster's eating a bun,
What fun!

**Isaac Shipp (8)**
**West Winch Primary School, King's Lynn**

## Am I Healthy?

Fruit and veg are good for me
Chocolate is bad, coming with sweets
I am like a boomerang but I do not come back to you
My last letter is A
I do go rotten and kids don't like me
I come from a country but not England
I am very healthy
I am good for snacks and picnics
I am a fruit.
What am I?

A: Banana.

**Ellie Florence (7)**
**Wicklewood Primary School, Wicklewood**

## Riddle Me Health

My first is in fish but not in pasta
My second is in fibre but not in salad
My third is in sausage but not in apple
My fourth is in calcium and in protein
My fifth is in carbohydrate and in healthy
You've got to eat me, please!

What am I?
A: Fruit.

**Finn Rigney (8)**
**Wicklewood Primary School, Wicklewood**

## Healthy Eating

My first is in dig and also in dog
My second is in an and also in wham
My third is in sing but not in rhythm
My fourth is in ray but not in way
My fifth is in yay and in day
Altogether I've got yoghurt in my group.
What am I?

A: Dairy.

**Phoebe Cohen (8)**
**Wicklewood Primary School, Wicklewood**

## Healthy Eating

My first is in Satsuma but not in orange.
My second is in apple and also in grape.
My third is in platter but not in fatter.
My fourth isn't in plum but is in carrot.
My fifth is in dragon fruit but not in passion fruit.
I'm made with lots of lettuce.
What am I?

A: Salad.

**Bryony King (7)**
**Wicklewood Primary School, Wicklewood**

## Healthy Eating Riddle

My first is in dairy but not in fish
My second is in protein but not in chocolate
My third is in pizza but not in interesting
My fourth is in lettuce but not in chicken
My fifth is in carbohydrate but not in pasta
Please, please, tell me what I am.

What am I?
A: Apple.

**Leonie Read (8)**
**Wicklewood Primary School, Wicklewood**

## What Am I?

I swirl around in spirals
I am yummy in your tummy
With tomato sauce
I can be thin
And I can be long
I can be swirly and I can be strong
When I am not cooked
What am I?

**Charlotte Cooper (9)**
**Wicklewood Primary School, Wicklewood**

## Food

My first is in carbohydrate and also in dairy,
My second is in protein but in food as well,
My third is in sugar, also in fruit,
My fourth is in vegetables but not in salt,
My fifth is in healthy but not in straw,
My sixth is in nuts but not in chocolate,
My seventh is in turnip, also in fizzing up,
My eighth is in vitamins but not in minerals.

**Minnie Michlmayr (7)**
**Wicklewood Primary School, Wicklewood**

## Healthy Eating Riddle

My first is in pea and also in protein
My second is in apple and also in carrot
My third is in sand and in salad too
My fourth is in salt but not in dairy
My fifth is in healthy and also in fat
What am I?

A: Pasta.

**Emily Sully (8)**
**Wicklewood Primary School, Wicklewood**

## What Am I?

My first is in first but not in second.
My second is in red but not in blue.
My third is not in green but is in hue.
My next is in indigo but never in stew.
My last is a drink that sounds like Typhoo!

What am I?
A: Fruit.

**Rowan Holloway (8)**
**Wicklewood Primary School, Wicklewood**

## Riddle

My first is in protein but not in vitamin
My second is in calcium but not in chicken
My third is in salad but not in fruit
My fourth is in salt and in newt
My fifth is in fat and in gnat.
What am I?

A: Pasta.

**Hamish Jeffery (7)**
**Wicklewood Primary School, Wicklewood**

## Pasta

P asta is yummy because you can put cheese on it.
A scrumptious, yummy meal.
S ome cheese and ketchup is fine too.
T o eat the yummiest thing on Earth.
A starter to go with it.
What am I?

A: Pasta.

**Jenson Holloway (7)**
**Wicklewood Primary School, Wicklewood**

## Riddle

My first is in peach and cabbage.
My second is in grapes and in pear.
My third is in pineapple and in grapefruit.
My fourth is in liquid and also in milk.
My fifth is in egg and also in boiled.
What am I?

A: Apple.

**Libby Lambert (8)**
**Wicklewood Primary School, Wicklewood**

## I Am Healthy

My first is in flare and twice in alarm
My second is in pear and also in pearl
My third is in parliament but not in ride
My fourth is in licence and also in life cycle
My last is in eager and also in eczema.
What am I?

A: Apple.

**James Vincent (7)**
**Wicklewood Primary School, Wicklewood**

## Riddle

My first is in protein and in pea and in pair.
My second is in eggs and in fear.
My third is in peach and in carrot and in cabbage.
My fourth is in carrot and in radish.
What am I?

A: Pear.

**Louise Goodings (7)**
**Wicklewood Primary School, Wicklewood**

## Riddle

It is all shapes and sizes.
It is dried or it can be fresh.
It is all sorts of colours.
It can be circular or wobbly.
What is it?

A: Pasta.

**Hannah Spratling (7)**
**Wicklewood Primary School, Wicklewood**

## The Beach

Running beside the sea, excited, splashing,
Waves crashing on the rocks and walls,
Children playing, building sandcastles with golden sand,
Soon to be washed away.
Fish and chips beside the beach with seagulls in the sky,
Soggy seaweed fresh from the sea, hiding in the rock,
Soft sand under my feet, walking through the golden sand,
Stony, sharp sand on the beach, poking at my feet as I walk by.
Having ice cream beside the beach with seagulls looking for food to steal,
I'm swimming with salty water in my mouth,
Waves smashing the sand and groynes,
Skin shining in the golden sun,
Colourful huts on the side of the beach,
Fresh air blowing away in the wind,
Some seagulls playing in the air like children.

**Katie Rodwell (7)**
**Wilby CE (VC) Primary School, Wilby**

## The Fight

Walking down the street, minding my own business,
A shove?
Fury flares within me,
Shocked, another punch,
There the man stands.
He throws another.
Infuriated, I throw a punch,
Angry I kick him in the shins.
Scared, I see a policeman!
Breathless, he punches the wind out of me,
Ashen-faced I quickly headbutt him.
The terrible fight ends,
Victorious,
Wary, he's gonna do it again.
Bewildered, have I hurt him?
Silly, I've really hurt this man.
Sadly I start to walk home.
I get to the gate in front of my house,
Embarrassment fills me,
My mind screams to run away,
I can't.
Afraid,
Unsure of myself, I go through the gate,
Ashamed and sad, I go inside.

**William Haigh (8)**
**Wilby CE (VC) Primary School, Wilby**

## The Beach

Mini skyscrapers stretching out to sea keeping sand still,
White horses galloping onto the beach,
Seagulls bobbing on the sea looking for fish,
Children building tall sandcastles with high walls,
Thundering waves washing up on the beach,
Wind roaring, groaning like a lion,
Stinky seaweed, stinky like cheesy feet,
Sea salt rubbing on my legs like sand,
Sand rushing through my feet as I'm sprinting to the sea,
Disgusting salt in my mouth, swimming.

**Sam Morris (9)**
**Wilby CE (VC) Primary School, Wilby**

## Churchyard Cat

I can taste delicious black chicken, yummy in my tummy,
Blackbirds eating seeds off the ground as I get low and stalk.
Suddenly, I pounce like a baby tiger
And I am rewarded with a baby blackbird.
Sad, tired, weak, missed an opportunity for a mouse meal,
Massive trees twenty times as big as me,
Crawl away in case one falls like a skyscraper.
Jumping in and out the flowers, dashing and darting,
It smells like nectar floating past my nose.
Graves perfect for scratching posts,
Not noticing the ghost coming from behind,
Frightened and shocked, I dash back to the church and hide inside.
Church bells ringing, *ding-dong, ding-dong*, hurts my ears,
Run to the top of the tree.
Bark, brown like soil, gets stuck in my feet,
Plodding along when suddenly I tread on a thistle, itchy and scratchy.
Lovely moss shaped like a circle,
Just like a bed to snuggle into and to go to bed.

**Tomas Earl (9)**
**Wilby CE (VC) Primary School, Wilby**

## Churchyard Cat

Squirrels pouncing about in the tree above,
Beautiful bird cheeping softly in the green and brown trees,
Ow! I've stepped on my tail,
Everything's so tall compared to me down below,
Lovely flowers catch my attention as they waft past my nose,
Graves; different shapes and different sizes,
Argh! The barking of a dog . . . *off a lead!*
Lovely green moss peeking through the grass,
I've found a warm spot just under a tree, *zzz.*
Cars zooming past and making me shiver,
Damp grass which my paws are on,
Birds' nests up in the tree which I try to climb, but I fail,
I lap up all the fresh water from the grass,
All the red berries fall apart in my mouth,
Oh, the lovely taste of *mouse meat!*
As I go home, I feel proud of myself.

**Louis Strehlow (8)**
**Wilby CE (VC) Primary School, Wilby**

## Churchyard Cat

Flowers and trees surrounding all around us,
Rabbit burrows everywhere on the green, wet ground,
Trees everywhere, surrounding us like a cage,
Flower petals everywhere on the ground and on people's graves,
Squirrels prancing tree to tree,
Chickens pecking at the wet, juicy grass,
I hear mice squeaking and running on the grass,
Birds tweeting in the tall churchyard trees,
Squirrels look for nuts and crack them with their teeth,
Smelling the fresh, juicy mice all around us,
The sweet smell of the flowers on people's graves,
I feel the wet grass tickling my toes as I am crawling,
As I walk on the stony path, they prick my paws,
I taste the blood of chickens and mice in my mouth,
The taste of mice is on the end of my tongue,
Leaping into the trees to get that squirrel taste in my mouth,
Feeling the crackly leaves under my paws,
I scratch my paws on the bark of the trees.

**Isla Whittle (8)**
**Wilby CE (VC) Primary School, Wilby**

## Churchyard Cat

Squirrels bouncing from branch to branch
As fast as a bullet.
Clucking chickens pecking for worms like lawnmowers,
I smell the beautiful yew trees from miles away.
Wet grass rushes straight through my paws.
Big gravestones stick out of the ground,
As tall as a giraffe.
I hear the bell of the school as the children line up.
I smell all the animals from here and there
And even when they've passed by.
The taste of beautiful mice in my mouth,
I hear chatting from the church as they pray.
I feel crispy leaves on my paws,
I see all the nature that Mother Nature has given us,
I smell creepy-crawlies from up and down,
I try to catch them.

**Shannon Curtis (9)**
**Wilby CE (VC) Primary School, Wilby**

## The Cat

Creepy gravestones in the graveyard,
As I am searching for juicy mice.
Wet, silky, green grass on my tiny paws,
Prickly leaves, while I creep through the bushes,
Walking, searching for mice and juicy birds
In their sticky birds' nests.
Brown, yucky mud goes on my soft feet.
Excited, happy, joyful, catching chickens in the churchyard.
Howling dogs chasing me around the graveyard,
While songs are being sung inside.
Spiky hedgehogs in prickly bushes,
Hibernating from the cold winter.
Hungry, starving for food, hunting in the graveyard
And birds squawking high.
The tall church, taller than me and other people,
Tired of running through the graveyard and fields,
Tiny mice in holes, trying to catch them,
I fall asleep in my basket.

**Liam Irvine (8)**
**Wilby CE (VC) Primary School, Wilby**

## Churchyard Cat

Birds tweeting, waiting for my paws to eat,
Chickens clucking on the pile of leaves, searching,
Leaves falling gracefully in the air, waiting to fall,
Grass growing smooth like silk under my paws,
Wind swirling round and round behind my tail,
Graves everywhere, massive like trees,
Trees surrounding me like green clouds,
Glass windows right in front of me like frozen water,
Feathers circle round and round,
Flowers lying on graves to give respect,
Scents of birds' feathers on the ground,
Branches whacking my face and paws,
Paws being dragged through the grass all wet,
Leaves crinkling underneath me,
Water lapping down my throat.

**Alice Evans-Hendrick (9)**
**Wilby CE (VC) Primary School, Wilby**

## Churchyard Cat

I taste bird pie in my mouth like the taste of Heaven,
Making my mouth water.
I am walking through the bush
And feeling brambles pricking my paws.
I pounce out of the bush,
Landing on the mouse and killing it!
I wait to get ready, I pounce on the chicken.
It struggles, I dig my claws into it.
I look around and see a big stone sticking out of the ground
With writing on it.
Grass soft and wet.
I hear dogs barking, making me scared.
I run away and creep in a bush.
I lie down and when the dog goes away,
I creep in the corner of the bush.
I sneak out of the bush
And try to recover from the shock.

**Lewis Roughton (7)**
**Wilby CE (VC) Primary School, Wilby**

## The Fight

Walking down the street minding my own business,
Suddenly I feel a punch. Who did that?
The man is running off,
The anger builds up inside me.
I throw a punch!
He was strong, but I was stronger,
He took the breath out of me,
I am frightened, what do I do?
I am relieved, the fight is over,
Victorious!
Sore and breathless.
Silly that I hit the man,
Petrified he will come back,
Frightened my mum or dad will find out,
Disobedient, I got into a fight,
Unhappy, I injured the man.
Regret.

**Jessie Evans-Hendrick (8)**
**Wilby CE (VC) Primary School, Wilby**

## Churchyard Cat

Silky grass runs through my paws as I prance through the churchyard,
Clucking chickens are pecking in the bushes, having fun,
I smell the animals that have passed away,
Tall grey things are striking out of the ground,
I hear the people chatting in the church,
I'm scared of dogs, barking as loudly as can be,
Tasting lovely, luxury mice in my mouth that I have caught,
Loud bells ring in the church,
I hear the trees swaying in the wind,
I feel the crunchy leaves as I walk through them,
I hit my head on the church, I'm not looking the right way,
I touch the wet bark as I climb up a tree,
I hear the leaves falling off the trees,
I smell the flowers on the ground,
I see the top of the tall church covered in rooks.

**Arwen Maguire (7)**
**Wilby CE (VC) Primary School, Wilby**

## The Fight

Walking sadly, minding my own business,
A push, he pushed me!
Who was that?
Suddenly I turned around,
A scary man, he throws a punch,
I throw punches back.
He pulls my hat down, I am scared.
He pushes me on the ground,
I was strongest.
He had blood streaming out of him,
He was walking away into the misty distance.
I walked home in a temper,
Wondering what my mum would say.
I got home . . .

**Alice Wiseman (8)**
**Wilby CE (VC) Primary School, Wilby**

## Churchyard Cat

Squirrels bouncing from tree to tree,
Bugs moving in the grass,
Trees swinging gracefully,
Dogs barking at me,
Dewdrops dripping from the grass,
Gravel between my toes,
Old footprints in the gravel,
Strange smells of flowers,
Soft grass beneath my toes,
Big stones sticking out of the ground,
A strong breeze,
I feel hungry,
I finally find somewhere to rest, then I sleep, cold skin.

**Jasmine Irvine (8)**
**Wilby CE (VC) Primary School, Wilby**

## The Graveyard

I see leaves scattered on the ground,
A squirrel runs fast to its hole in the tree,
Chickens, big, small, middle-sized, red, ginger, black and grey,
Birds singing and tweeting like cats calling to their mothers,
Mice scattering across the grass,
Animals entering and crawling over the graves,
Smell of dead flowers sweeping to my nose,
Dead, soggy grass, thistles and nettles brush past my legs,
I touch the grass, green and growing,
Catch up with a mouse and taste it, yum, yum, yum,
Bark on the trees like spiky thorns as I climb,
Stones in my claws, wet with dew.

**Alice Mills (8)**
**Wilby CE (VC) Primary School, Wilby**

## Churchyard Cat

Lots of humungous graves sticking out of the ground,
Hedgehogs rustling in the autumn leaves,
Birds' nests high in the tree,
Chilly wind flies through my whiskers,
I lay like a tunnel so mice go in my mouth,
Soft, spongy grass under my paws,
Water splashing out of puddles,
Rats, mice, birds all over the giant place,
Juicy mice and birds scatter droppings,
Birds tweeting high in the sky,
I climb a tree and swipe at a bird,
Rustles in the leaves as I leap onto a mouse!

**Eddie Shearman (8)**
**Wilby CE (VC) Primary School, Wilby**

## Churchyard Cat

Spiky thistles prick my paws as I stalk the graveyard,
Stalking on soft and spongy grass,
Rough bark under my paws as I cling onto the tree,
While clinging onto the tree I hear birds tweeting,
Leaves rustling and dogs barking in the distance.
Coming down the tree, almost falling, finally feeling the ground,
Suddenly, a gust of cold wind brushes through my whiskers,
I smell rats and mice all over the giant churchyard,
Fresh whiffs of mice all over the ground.
Loads of old, enormous, funny stones sticking out of the ground,
Fresh water from a puddle by the gates,
Soon walk home on the fence.

**Xander Redgrave (9)**
**Wilby CE (VC) Primary School, Wilby**

## The Churchyard Cat

Leaves scattered on the ground,
Some chickens big, grey and ginger,
I hear birds singing and tweeting in the blue sky,
Soon there were some mice scattering on the green grass,
Then I hear dogs barking at the cats in the house,
I smell dead flowers sweeping to my nose,
But then I smell soggy grass in the air,
The green grass growing in the sun,
Old stones everywhere and chickens peering at them,
I catch a juicy mouse and taste it,
Then I feel the bark of the tree sharp on my paws.

**Abbie Hawes (9)**
**Wilby CE (VC) Primary School, Wilby**

## The Cat

Gravestones as still as statues,
Tiny mice, fat and juicy, like the taste of heaven, a luxury dinner,
I can hear howling dogs in the fields,
Brown, yucky mud squelching in between my paws,
Wet, soggy grass goes through my paws as I hunt for food,
As I climb up the trees, the sticky bird's nest sticks to my fur.
I can hear songs getting sung in the church.
As I creep up on my prey in the prickly bushes,
The leaves itch my fur.
Spiky hedgehogs hibernating under the leaves,
Squawking birds in the sky, searching for food.

**Henry Bishop (7)**
**Wilby CE (VC) Primary School, Wilby**

## Churchyard Cat

Silky grass between my toes,
Rough, stony gravel painful on my paws,
As I walk I start to feel hungry,
I wander around, looking for food,
But as I walk looking for food,
Mud squelches on my paws,
Walking slowly, scared in case dogs pounce out,
I hear growling in the air,
There stands the dog in front of me,
I try to run away and there stands a juicy mouse.

**Emily Bullock (9)**
**Wilby CE (VC) Primary School, Wilby**

## The Beach

Beach huts colourful like a straight rainbow on the ground,
Crushing of waves as they roar loudly,
Fish and chips frying, sizzling on the black stoves,
Seagulls squawking high in the sky,
People throwing bread out to seagulls,
Crabs and fish wash up on the shore,
Sand rushing through my hands and feet,
When I crush the seashells it makes a terrible noise.
I head home, remembering.

**Lily Strehlow (8)**
**Wilby CE (VC) Primary School, Wilby**

## Churchyard Cat

Squirrels running and prancing about,
Birds flapping in the air as they fly,
Wind blowing swiftly and silently,
Flowers are growing in the sunlight,
I am running, crouching on the floor,
Crawling on the damp, green grass,
All the plants growing, it's like heaven,
Sleeping under a tree.

**James Balls (7)**
**Wilby CE (VC) Primary School, Wilby**

## Maddie's Workshop

### Featured Author:
# Maddie Stewart

**Maddie is a children's writer, poet and author who currently lives in Coney Island, Northern Ireland.**

Maddie has 5 published children's books, 'Cinders', 'Hal's Sleepover', 'Bertie Rooster', 'Peg' and 'Clever Daddy'. Maddie uses her own unpublished work to provide entertaining, interactive poems and rhyming stories for use in her workshops with children when she visits schools, libraries, arts centres and book festivals. Favourites are 'Silly Billy, Auntie Millie' and 'I'm a Cool, Cool Kid'. Maddie works throughout Ireland from her home in County Down. She is also happy to work from a variety of bases in England. She has friends and family, with whom she regularly stays, in Leicester, Bedford, London and Ashford (Kent). Maddie's workshops are aimed at 5-11-year-olds. Check out Maddie's website for all her latest news and free poetry resources **www.maddiestewart.com**.

*Read on to pick up some fab writing tips!*

# Nonsense Workshop

**If you find silliness fun, you will love nonsense poems. Nonsense poems might describe silly things, or people, or situations, or, any combination of the three.**

**For example:**

When I got out of bed today,
both my arms had run away.
I sent my feet to fetch them back.
When they came back, toe in hand
I realised what they had planned.
They'd made the breakfast I love most,
buttered spider's eggs on toast.

**One way to find out if you enjoy nonsense poems is to start with familiar nursery rhymes. Ask your teacher to read them out, putting in the names of some children in your class.**

Like this: Troy and Jill went up the hill
to fetch a pail of water.
Troy fell down
and broke his crown
and Jill came tumbling after.

**If anyone is upset at the idea of using their name, then don't use it.**

**Did you find this fun?**

# Maddie's Workshop

**Now try changing a nursery rhyme.
Keep the rhythm and the rhyme style, but invent a silly situation.**

Like this: Hickory Dickory Dare
a pig flew up in the air.
The clouds above
gave him a shove
Hickory Dickory Dare.

Or this: Little Miss Mabel
sat at her table
eating a strawberry pie
but a big, hairy beast
stole her strawberry feast
and made poor little Mabel cry.

**How does your rhyme sound if you put your own name in it?**

**Another idea for nonsense poems is to pretend letters are people and have them do silly things.**

For example:

| Mrs A | Mrs B | Mrs C |
| Lost her way | Dropped a pea | Ate a tree |

**To make your own 'Silly People Poem', think of a word to use.
To show you an example, I will choose the word 'silly'.
Write your word vertically down the left hand side of your page.
Then write down some words which rhyme
with the sound of each letter.**

**S** mess, dress, Bess, chess, cress
**I** eye, bye, sky, guy, pie, sky
**L** sell, bell, shell, tell, swell, well
**L** " " " " " " (" means the same as written above)
**Y** (the same words as those rhyming with I)

**Use your rhyming word lists to help you make up your poem.**

Mrs S made a mess
Mrs I ate a pie
Mrs L rang a bell
Mrs L broke a shell
Mrs Y said 'Bye-bye.'

**You might even make a 'Silly Alphabet' by using all the letters of the alphabet.**

**It is hard to find rhyming words for all the letters. H, X and W are letters which are hard to match with rhyming words. I'll give you some I've thought of:**

**H** - cage, stage, wage (close but not perfect)
**X** - flex, specs, complex, Middlesex
**W** - trouble you, chicken coop, bubble zoo

**However, with nonsense poems, you can use nonsense words. You can make up your own words.**

**To start making up nonsense words you could try mixing dictionary words together. Let's make up some nonsense animals.**

**Make two lists of animals. (You can include birds and fish as well.)**

**Your lists can be as long as you like. These are lists I made:**

| | |
|---|---|
| elephant | kangaroo |
| tiger | penguin |
| lizard | octopus |
| monkey | chicken |

**Now use the start of an animal on one list and substitute it for the start of an animal from your other list.**

I might use the start of oct/opus ... oct and substitute it for the end of l/izard to give me a new nonsense animal ... an octizard.
I might swap the start of monk/ey ... monk with the end of kang/aroo
To give me another new nonsense animal ... a monkaroo.

**What might a monkaroo look like? What might it eat?**

**You could try mixing some food words in the same way, to make up nonsense foods.**

| | |
|---|---|
| cabbage | potatoes |
| lettuce | parsley |
| bacon | crisps |

**Cribbage, bacley, and lettatoes are some nonsense foods made up from my lists.**

**Let's see if I can make a nonsense poem about my monkaroo.**

# Maddie's Workshop

> My monkaroo loves bacley.
> He'll eat lettatoes too
> But his favourite food is cribbage
> Especially if it's blue.

**Would you like to try and make up your own nonsense poem?**

**Nonsense words don't have to be a combination of dictionary words.
They can be completely 'made up'.
You can use nonsense words to write nonsense sonnets,
or list poems or any type of poem you like.**

**Here is a poem full of nonsense words:**

> I melly micked a turdle
> and flecked a pendril's tum.
> I plotineyed a shugat
> and dracked a pipin's plum.

**Ask your teacher to read it putting in some children's names instead
of the first I, and he or she instead of the second I.**

**Did that sound funny?**

You might think that nonsense poems are just silly and not for the serious poet. However poets tend to love language. Making up your own words is a natural part of enjoying words and sounds and how they fit together. Many poets love the freedom nonsense poems give them. Lots and lots of very famous poets have written nonsense poems. I'll name some: **Edward Lear**, **Roger McGough**, **Lewis Carroll**, **Jack Prelutsky** and **Nick Toczek**. Can you or your teacher think of any more? For help with a class nonsense poem or to find more nonsense nursery rhymes look on my website, **www.maddiestewart.com**. Have fun! Maddie Stewart.

# Poetry Techniques

## Here is a selection of poetry techniques with examples

### Metaphors & Similes

A *metaphor* is when you describe your subject *as* something else, for example:
'Winter is a cruel master leaving the servants in a bleak wilderness'
whereas a *simile* describes your subject *like* something else i.e.
'His blue eyes are like ice-cold puddles' or 'The flames flickered like eyelashes'.

### Personification

This is to simply give a personality to something that is not human, for example
'Fear spreads her uneasiness around' or 'Summer casts down her warm sunrays'.

### Imagery

To use words to create mental pictures of what you are trying to convey,
your poem should awaken the senses and make the reader
feel like they are in that poetic scene …
'The sky was streaked with pink and red as shadows
cast across the once-golden sand'.
'The sea gently lapped the shore as the palm trees rustled softly
in the evening breeze'.

### Assonance & Alliteration

*Alliteration* uses a repeated constant sound and this effect can be quite striking:
'Smash, slippery snake slithered sideways'.
*Assonance* repeats a significant vowel or vowel sound to create an impact:
'The pool looked cool'.

# Poetry Techniques

## Repetition

By repeating a significant word the echo effect can be a very powerful way of enhancing an emotion or point your poem is putting across.

'The blows rained down, down,
Never ceasing,
Never caring
About the pain,
The pain'.

## Onomatopoeia

This simply means you use words that sound like the noise you are describing, for example 'The rain *pattered* on the window' or 'The tin can *clattered* up the alley'.

## Rhythm & Metre

The *rhythm* of a poem means 'the beat', the sense of movement you create. The placing of punctuation and the use of syllables affect the *rhythm* of the poem.
If your intention is to have your poem read slowly, use double, triple or larger syllables and punctuate more often, where as if you want to have a fast-paced read use single syllables, less punctuation and shorter sentences.
If you have a regular rhythm throughout your poem this is known as *metre*.

## Enjambment

This means you don't use punctuation at the end of your line, you simply let the line flow on to the next one. It is commonly used and is a good word to drop into your homework!

## Tone & Lyric

The poet's intention is expressed through their *tone*. You may feel happiness, anger, confusion, loathing or admiration for your poetic subject. Are you criticising or praising? How you feel about your topic will affect your choice of words and therefore your *tone*. For example 'I *loved* her', 'I *cared* for her', 'I *liked* her'.
If you write the poem from a personal view or experience this is referred to as a *lyrical* poem. A good example of a lyrical poem is Seamus Heaney's 'Mid-term Break' or any sonnet!

# All About Shakespeare

### Try this fun quiz with your family, friends or even in class!

**1. Where was Shakespeare born?**

...........................................................................................................................

**2. Mercutio is a character in which Shakepeare play?**

...........................................................................................................................

**3. Which monarch was said to be 'quite a fan' of his work?**

...........................................................................................................................

**4. How old was he when he married?**

...........................................................................................................................

**5. What is the name of the last and 'only original' play he wrote?**

...........................................................................................................................

**6. What are the names of King Lear's three daughters?**

...........................................................................................................................

**7. Who is Anne Hathaway?**

...........................................................................................................................

# All About Shakespeare

8. Which city is the play 'Othello' set in?

..................................................................................................................

9. Can you name 2 of Shakespeare's 17 comedies?

..................................................................................................................

10. 'This day is call'd the feast of Crispian: He that outlives this day, and comes safe home, Will stand a tip-toe when this day is nam'd, and rouse him at the name of Crispian' is a quote from which play?

..................................................................................................................

11. Leonardo DiCaprio played Romeo in the modern day film version of Romeo and Juliet. Who played Juliet in the movie?

..................................................................................................

12. Three witches famously appear in which play?

..................................................................................................................

13. Which famous Shakespearean character is Eric in the image to the left?

..................................................................................................

14. What was Shakespeare's favourite poetic form?

..................................................................................................................

**Answers are printed on the last page of the book, good luck!**

**If you would rather try the quiz online,
you can do so at www.youngwriters.co.uk.**

# Poetry Activity

## Word Soup

**To help you write a poem, or even a story, on any theme, you should create word soup!**

If you have a theme or subject for your poem, base your word soup on it. If not, don't worry, the word soup will help you find a theme.

**To start your word soup you need ingredients:**

- Nouns (names of people, places, objects, feelings, i.e. Mum, Paris, house, anger)
- Colours
- Verbs ('doing words', i.e. kicking, laughing, running, falling, smiling)
- Adjectives (words that describe nouns, i.e. tall, hairy, hollow, smelly, angelic)

We suggest at least 5 of each from the above list, this will make sure your word soup has plenty of choice. Now, if you have already been given a theme or title for your poem, base your ingredients on this. If you have no idea what to write about, write down whatever you like, or ask a teacher or family member to give you a theme to write about.

# Poetry Activity

## Making Word Soup

Next, you'll need a sheet of paper.
Cut it into at least 20 pieces. Make sure the pieces are big enough to write your ingredients on, one ingredient on each piece of paper.
Write your ingredients on the pieces of paper.
Shuffle the pieces of paper and put them all in a box or bowl
- something you can pick the paper out of without looking at the words.
Pick out 5 words to start and use them to write your poem!

### Example:

Our theme is winter. Our ingredients are:
- Nouns: snowflake, Santa, hat, Christmas, snowman.
- Colours: blue, white, green, orange, red.
- Verbs: ice-skating, playing, laughing, smiling, wrapping.
- Adjectives: cold, tall, fast, crunchy, sparkly.

**Our word soup gave us these 5 words:
snowman, red, cold, hat, fast and our poem goes like this:**

It's a *cold* winter's day,
My nose and cheeks are *red*
As I'm outside, building my *snowman*,
I add a *hat* and a carrot nose to finish,
I hope he doesn't melt too *fast*!

**Tip: add more ingredients to your word soup
and see how many different poems you can write!**

**Tip: if you're finding it hard to write a poem with
the words you've picked, swap a word with another one!**

**Tip: try adding poem styles and techniques,
such as assonance or haiku to your soup for an added challenge!**

# Young Writers Information

We hope you have enjoyed reading this book - and that you will continue to enjoy it in the coming years.

If you like reading and writing poetry drop us a line, or give us a call, and we'll send you a free information pack.

Alternatively, if you would like to order further copies of this book or any of our other titles, then please give us a call or log onto our website at www.youngwriters.co.uk.

Young Writers Information
Remus House
Coltsfoot Drive
Peterborough
PE2 9BF
Tel: (01733) 890066
Fax: (01733) 313524

Email: info@youngwriters.co.uk

## Shakespeare Quiz Answers

**1.** Stratford-upon-Avon **2.** Romeo and Juliet **3.** James I **4.** 18 **5.** The Tempest **6.** Regan, Cordelia and Goneril **7.** His wife **8.** Venice **9.** All's Well That Ends Well, As You Like It, The Comedy of Errors, Cymbeline, Love's Labour's Lost, Measure for Measure, The Merchant of Venice, The Merry Wives of Windsor, A Midsummer Night's Dream, Much Ado About Nothing, Pericles - Prince of Tyre, The Taming of the Shrew, The Tempest, Twelfth Night, The Two Gentlemen of Verona, Troilus & Cressida, The Winter's Tale **10.** Henry V **11.** Claire Danes **12.** Macbeth **13.** Hamlet **14.** Sonnet